Ending My Silence

Rising Above Sexual and Emotional Abuse

Lydia Lin

Copyright © 2019 Lydia Lin

All rights reserved. No part of this publication may be reproduced, distributed, or transmitted in any form or by any means, including photocopying, recording, or other electronic or mechanical methods, without the prior written permission of the publisher, except in the case of brief quotations embodied in reviews and certain other non-commercial uses permitted by copyright law.

ISBN: 978-1-7338341-0-0

Acknowledgments

I'm eternally grateful to my best friend George, my life coach Aabri, my publishing coach Lise, my therapist Mindy and other mental health care professionals to help me recover from my traumatic past enough to be able to write this book. This book would not have been possible without your support. Thank you for continuing to believe in me and encourage me.

To all my launch team friends, thank you for reading, reviewing, and supporting me. I thank you from the bottom of my heart.

Author's Note

"Ending My Silence" is a true story. However, names of individuals have been changed.

Trigger warning: This book contains content that may be distressing. Do not read if you can't handle the mention of rape or suicide.

Also, just because certain therapy methods worked for me does not mean they will work for anyone else dealing with similar trauma. If you are in need of therapy, please seek professional help.

Table of Contents

Acknowledgments 3
Author's Note 4
Chapter 1 8
Chapter 2 18
Chapter 3 25
Chapter 4 29
Chapter 5 37
Chapter 6 43
Chapter 7 46
Chapter 8 51
Chapter 9 55
Chapter 10 58
Chapter 11 62
Chapter 12 65
Chapter 13 69
Chapter 14 73
Chapter 15 75
Chapter 16 77
Chapter 17 78
Chapter 18 79
Chapter 19 84

Chapter 20	86
Chapter 21	92
Chapter 22	95
Chapter 23	99
Chapter 24	102
Chapter 25	113
Chapter 26	117
Chapter 27	119
Chapter 28	125
Chapter 29	128
Chapter 30	130
Chapter 31	132
Chapter 32	133
Chapter 33	135
Chapter 34	138
Chapter 35	143
Chapter 36	146
Chapter 37	152
Chapter 38	156
Chapter 39	159
Chapter 40	163
Chapter 41	165
Chapter 42	168
Chapter 43	170

Chapter 44 173

Chapter 45 176

Chapter 46 178

Chapter 47 180

Chapter 48 183

Chapter 49 185

Chapter 50 187

Chapter 51 192

Chapter 52 195

Chapter 53 200

Chapter 54 203

Chapter 55 207

Chapter 56 210

Chapter 57 212

Chapter 58 217

Chapter 59 222

Chapter 60 224

Chapter 61 234

Chapter 62 238

Chapter 63 244

Chapter 64 248

Chapter 65 250

Epilogue 253

1

I hadn't learned the word "rape" until several months after it had happened to me. I remember screaming until I had no voice left to scream with; fighting with all my muscles until I felt like I was just meat—just a slab of a person, a body lying on the hotel room bed. I remember all the white walls of that small room seeming to come down on me, with nowhere to escape. I remember lying there spread-eagled, not wanting to move. I didn't want to touch myself by accident, didn't want to remember the sensation of his skin on mine, scraping into me with bruising force. I remember the cool white sheets on the hotel room bed. They were even colder now and wet with messy bloodstains—evidence of my failed resistance. He wanted to make sure I saw them so that I'd remember, but I didn't want to see.

My day started like any other day in what I considered as ordinary senior year student high-school days in Beijing, China. I was a robot of a good student; I earned mostly A's, studied hard, played little, went to bed consistently by 11pm and woke up every day by 7am.

Mom and Dad had raised me to never hang out with friends Monday through Thursday so that I could focus on my studies. I rarely procrastinated for fear of receiving another tongue lashing—those happened frequently enough that I tried my best to avoid additional parental ire with what little of my life I could control. There were plenty of rules and tasks to living in Mom and Dad's household, and you had hell to pay if they were broken.

There wasn't much time to think beyond the life that I lived every day, what with Mom and Dad considering free time to be evil and unacceptable. Safety was in hugging a book—preferably a textbook—which served as the occasional shield of protection from the line of fire. But none of this really bothered me; this was my "normal".

I had become accustomed to Mom and Dad's strictly enforced regiment since elementary school. And so, I'm sure I went to school that day, did my homework, and all the other normal things in my Spartan routine. Another normal thing in my day was that Mom and Dad yelled at me, called me some hurtful names, or snarled some scathing things.

On rare occasions, they would say something more extreme. Occasionally, before I had even turned ten, I remember a few times where Dad was very angry and threatened to throw me in a ditch and leave me to die there. Or Mom might wail that I was the reason her life was shit. Afterwards they would explain everything away with an old Chinese idiom, "打是亲，骂是爱" (da shi qin, ma shi ai). This saying roughly translated justified abuse as a form of deep, familial love. It claimed that you were only beaten and verbally abused because your family cared about you so, so much.

Most of the time, I would do my best to filter out or numb myself to their words. What protected me most though, was that in large part, I believed what they said about me. If they called me things such as "stupid" or "worthless", those were no longer insults, but merely facts. It was like being told that my hair was black, and my hair IS black.

In senior year, Mom and Dad were more abusive than usual. I was soon to be "leaving the nest" and going to America for college. Equally—

if not more troubling for them—was that I was in a romantic relationship that they strongly disapproved of. Dad actually threatened to hire some thugs to beat up my boyfriend. This threat carried some weight since it was indeed possible, or at least, so I believed. Mom even believed the threat enough that she talked Dad out of the idea each time by going over all the legal consequences that might have.

I think another reason that made Mom and Dad more toxic than usual was that I was starting to develop some independent thoughts and personality, whereas in the past, I had rarely expressed any. I was starting to believe that I wasn't all of the negative things Mom and Dad claimed were true about me.

Fueled by my boyfriend, I no longer was content to accept all their insults as fact. They said I was worthless and he said I was amazing. I believed neither party, but felt that I was somewhere in between. I was going through that phase of growing up where parents were no longer gods. They were no longer able to completely define me without my thinking about it at least. Through their harsh parenting, they had successfully delayed my realizing this until senior year of high school, but here I was beginning to think on my own. In response to my rebellion, Mom and Dad simply ramped up the abuse, thinking it would crush me and things would go back to the way things had been. It was a painful time.

After the day's painful tongue-lashing, I'd hold on to my tears until I got to hang out with Yi, my boyfriend and closest friend. He was my first ever boyfriend, and very special to me. He was gentle and kind and I strongly believed that his was the only shoulder that I could cry on.

We couldn't be more different. He was several years older than me, twenty-seven to my eighteen. He had been working for several years, where I was still a student and hadn't yet held an actual job. I was American-born with English as my first language, and he was a Chinese-born Chinese man who only spoke Chinese. He had gone to Chinese public schools for education, where I had mostly attended international schools. But despite our vast differences, I knew I had strong feelings and attachment to him. This was more based on emotional need than love. He was the first person that I had really opened up to about the things Mom and Dad yelled at me. He was the first person refuting all the terrible things Mom and Dad had called me. He was the first person who inspired me to dream of a better life.

So, just like any other day that I could get away from the house, I went to him. Maybe we met at his place then went to the hotel, or maybe I just went directly to the hotel. I don't remember where the date started that day. We had to meet at hotels because his room was so saturated in the smell of his cigarette smoking habit that I couldn't breathe. He was tired from his day at work, so he was relaxing on the bed with his arms folded. I sat on the only chair in the small, cheap hotel room he had gotten us for the night. I wept and raged to him about all the bad things Mom and Dad had called me that day. We had done this enough times that he was no longer surprised to hear Mom and Dad's descriptions of me. Although I was not allowed to stay out overnight, I had recently begun to break this rule, since Mom and Dad's behavior was driving me out of the house and out of my mind.

Eventually, Yi had heard enough and picked me up out of the seat and brought me to lie down on the bed next to him. Being much stronger than me—a result of his near daily habit of working out by boxing—he always picked me up like it was nothing and I loved it. It made me feel safe and protected, and like those happy children who are picked up and twirled around in movies in slow motion.

He wrapped me up in his lean but powerfully muscled arms to soothe some of the hurt. Mumbling into my hair, he mused aloud about his dream of taking me away from them so they couldn't hurt me anymore.

It was a game of make-believe we'd play, or so I thought. A make-believe future where Mom and Dad weren't there to call me "whore", "trash", "waste of money", "waste of life", or other things. It was a game I enjoyed.

I don't know if he really thought it might happen. Maybe he truly thought I'd marry him and we'd elope somewhere and start new lives. I just used our make-believe game to cope with the abuse. In my mind, the cure to my pain was surviving by any means possible until 5 months from today. I already knew I'd get on a plane then and go to the US to start college. I would be flying away from anything, everyone, everything that I ever knew. I thought of this as a chance to start over and create a life with less pain and more freedom. It was fun to talk about—my little light at the end of the tunnel.

Yi shifted me and started stroking my body. This wasn't unfamiliar yet. He had explained to me before that he and other males enjoyed this kind of physical contact. I was happy to let him caress me just for giving me a shoulder to cry on. He whispered some warm, fuzzy things and that was nice. I rarely heard nice words about me from my family, and even less so this year. Over the course of just a few months, Yi had thoroughly convinced me he loved me more and better than Mom and Dad did. Plus, he knew me better than they did. Dad didn't know my size of clothes; Mom didn't know any of my favorite things, and Yi knew it all.

We'd lain down before like this, even without clothes once, but we always stopped, and I felt safe with the pace of things. Over time and each time, he had brought me a little further along the physical side of things, but I was not yet alarmed. I trusted him.

Although I could not understand his enjoyment of physical things, I did want to make him happy as he made me happy. So, it did not bother me to follow his instructions. I saw no harm in what we were doing and he never asked me to do anything I was incapable of, so I typically did what he asked me to do. I wanted him to like me and keep liking me. I couldn't admit it to myself, but in truth I was terrified of losing him. To me, he was the only thing keeping me afloat.

I closed my eyes and breathed deeply, his arm under my cheek, his deeper chest breathing next to mine. I just bathed in that warmth for a moment, emptying my mind of all the hurt from the world. His shirt was soft, but I wrinkled my nose at the permanent scent of cigarette smoke that clung to his body and clothing.

But today, he wanted more and I didn't know what that meant. We hadn't talked about sex too much before; I'd always blush and change the subject. Honestly, the concept horrified me. Even though I somewhat regularly kissed him, I felt no physical pleasure in the activity whatsoever. I kissed him purely as I thought a girlfriend should do. I was fulfilling my role and function. I also did not understand physical arousal or pleasure, not having experienced it yet myself. I did not feel pent up in any physical or sexual way and I could not understand the sexual desire he talked about sometimes.

Looking back, I know now that I was just not ready for sex with anybody. Although I was technically eighteen and legal, my mind had not developed interest in that kind of stuff. I lacked the curiosity, the maturity, the desire. He was nine years older than me, and a guy. We were just too different, but there was no way I could anticipate what was going to happen. I was too naïve and too innocent to notice any danger signs, since I didn't even know what a danger sign looked like.

He positioned himself on top of me fast and kissed me harder than he'd kissed me before. Confused, I thought he was just showing me a new way to kiss. Although somewhat panicked, I still trusted him and so tried to copy his new hard kissing technique. I mirrored and parroted back as he had encouraged me to do before with other kinds of kissing and petting. I made sure to close my eyes, because he had told me never to kiss with your eyes open.

His body felt too hot, his skin felt like it was burning under my cold fingertips. His breathing was a little more unsteady than I'd heard before. I didn't know what any of that meant.

He took off my pants and socks.

I remember the room was dark except for some weak street light outside the window. I remember I was wearing my white undies. They were very plain, ugly even, but I liked them because they were very comfortable. They were full coverage with just the tiniest bit of a lace edge to it, the lace edge being so tiny as to be invisible, especially in the dark of the room. To me they also symbolized safety. Surely Yi would not be turned on by these boring panties. Surely, he would not be interested in the physical side of things.

To my surprise, Yi gripped the side of my panties and began to tug them off. I didn't want to surrender them so he roughly tore my shirt off despite my confused protests. I tried to use a playful tone to diffuse his weirdly violent vibe that he was giving off before I realized he wasn't talking anymore. He always talked me through and explained things, coached me in what to do. I opened my eyes.

He was already naked.

I shakily asked him what he was doing, but his arm strength was suddenly terrifying. I was pinned to the bed. And then my white panties were the only remaining article of clothing. I remember I believed until the moment he stripped them off me that they might protect me from his sexual hunger. Then, with his one hand painfully and powerfully squeezing my wrists together over my head, he leaned into me with more of his body weight. I struggled against him with no success; he was much heavier and stronger than me. I could feel how hard he was everywhere—his muscles flexed and tense, and he wasn't gentle, and he wasn't kind.

My body instinctively started putting up some more resistance, but I was still in denial over what was happening. Was this really the loving Yi, who listened to me prattle on about my high school life? This was the kind Yi, who held me when I cried? This was the hero Yi, who talked about fantasy stories of how he would take me far away and rescue me from Mom and Dad? Surely this was just an act, just a game; it was ending soon—this wasn't real.

I was breathing too fast as I tried to push away from him. His arms were suddenly steel-like. I couldn't cause them to budge at all. I flailed my legs, trying to slide away. The only way to go was up towards the headboard and perhaps wriggle free. I tried desperately to move away from him, but he wasn't going to let me go, and I learned the truth of our strength disparity.

I remembered all the previous times we had play-wrestled for fun, all those times he had let me win. I had giggled at the fun of it, but tonight, I was going to experience horror I'd never imagined possible. How was this happening? He was my friend, my best friend, my only confidante, the most trusted one, the only who was saving me from the hurts of the world. Now his naked body was an immovable cage around me, bruising me with the pressure he was exerting on my limbs so that I could not budge. I was looking anywhere for escape until he placed his hand on my neck and forced me to stare into his face.

[NO]

I don't remember when I started screaming. I probably started screaming before he even entered me. The moment he pushed into me, my world exploded into pain. Pain was all I could see, all I could hear, all I could feel. And I screamed as if I screamed loud enough, it would change the reality that was happening to me and around me. I screamed as if I could out-scream the pain that I was drowning in. I screamed as if someone would hear me and do something. I screamed and screamed and screamed and screamed until there were no more tears left, no muscles left, no voice left, but no one came.

I don't know how long he raped me. I know he destroyed me so thoroughly, that my body didn't have the strength to put up a fight when he started hurting me again. He raped me another five times that same night and into the early and then late morning hours. I was just a body. I was barely conscious enough to care about what he did or was doing. I felt like my body was not mine. I felt I was floating above and away from my body. I wanted to die.

When he was finally done, he casually and gently wiped the dried blood off of my inner thighs. He smirked at my prone form. I locked my eyes onto the end table, not wanting to see his eyes, his face, his body. I stared at the end table unblinking and unmoving, hoping that if I acted like I was dead, perhaps I would be dead.

What was I going to do now? Just as Mom and Dad repeated that they loved me and then hurt me, he had now done the same. Part of me hated what he had done, part of me didn't know how to survive without him. And what if these closest human beings to me were just how everyone else was? What if everyone else loved and hurt each other too, and this was just normal? What if this was wrong? What if it wasn't? My thoughts flew jaggedly in circles.

Between thoughts of Mom and Dad and him, I lost all hope for a moment. I imagined how wonderful it would be ending all the questioning by jumping off the roof of the hotel. I knew I wanted to wipe that smug, satisfied look from his face. I wanted to hurt Mom and Dad for hurting me for all these years. No one else would miss me or care.

Splattering all over the ground was sure to draw some kind of reaction from both parties. Maybe jumping was the only way to be free. Maybe killing myself was the only thing I had control or power over. But my body was too broken to move, and I fell into exhausted unconsciousness. This dark thought sunk into my subconscious to surface again and again over the years, but while I was asleep that night, I thought and dreamed nothing.

And that was my first time.

2

I remember the January before my 18th birthday. I sat down one day and decided I needed to experience a relationship. I didn't have a crush on anyone, nor had I ever had one, but I felt it would be wise to pick up some relationship experience. I wanted to experiment with a relationship while I still lived in the comfort and safety of Mom and Dad's home—just in case I had questions or something were to go wrong, I could reach out to them for help or hide in my room or something. I also felt a great deal of peer pressure since other students in school were in relationships. Plus, my younger brother had already been in a couple relationships and even had his first kiss.

Yes, I felt it was logical and smart to try this out here, at this time, when I had the most protection and safety net. After all, once I went to college, I would not have Mom and Dad around me. Everyone would be new and there would be no one to turn to if I had any questions.

Winter was particularly cold and lonely that year. My friends all left on their various family vacations. Since I had done quite well the previous semester and my brother was struggling academically and emotionally, Mom loaded him up with additional work and lavished upon him most of her worried attention. I was left to my own devices. All this meant that I was absolutely and totally bored, bored, bored.

Mom was busy tutoring my brother most of the day so that he could catch up in school. He was less and less interested in graduating, it would seem. His grades and attendance were slipping in equal measure. Mom was doing her best, sometimes even going so far as to complete assignments for him. It was like pulling teeth, getting my brother through school. Mom was worn thin taking care of everyone and taking special care of my brother, as she repeated many times to me. Dad was busy with work as usual, which left me with no friends, no brother, no parents. Who was I to have fun with?

Bored, bored, bored.

Mom, irritable already, found my restless presence at home to be distracting and counterproductive. In an exasperated attempt to get me out of her hair, Mom suggested that I go to the nearest ski range. A little north of Beijing there was a skiing place called Nanshan Ski Village. It didn't have a very big ski range, with only a few slopes and oftentimes not enough real snow for skiing. To compensate, they would pump man-made snow onto the slopes, which was far less forgiving to fall on, but good enough to use for snow sports.

I was very accustomed to taking lessons, so I welcomed the idea of having a skiing instructor coach me on how to ski. A few years ago, on a family vacation, we had gone to the northern part of China and I had experienced skiing for the first time. I had greatly enjoyed the single lesson I had had while we were there, but hadn't had an opportunity to develop this skill further since then.

Mom paid for an instructor to teach me at Nanshan. My instructor, an older man who skied seemingly effortlessly, was patient and good at coaching me. Before long, I found myself attempting the black diamond slope with him. He would ski gracefully behind me while shouting to remind me of when to do this or that thing. My leg muscles burned and my cheeks were red, but I became increasingly more confident on the slopes. A week later, my instructor announced that I no longer needed him to babysit me down the slope. I could practice the black diamond there without supervision.

Overjoyed, I announced my "graduation" to Mom and Dad and asked if I might have my own set of ski gear.

Since Mom and Dad were pleased with my school performance that semester, they agreed without much resistance. It was decided that my full set of ski gear was to be my reward and then some. I was so happy. Dragging my somewhat less-passionate Mom into the stores, we searched for a cool ski outfit, skis, and ski accessories. Numerous store salespeople anxiously tried to hold my attention and hopefully earn Mom and Dad's money.

The store at the very end of the street, and the one closest to the ski lift, had what I was looking for. I found a ski suit that was both light and warm, snazzy, and flexible. It had a white and black checkered pattern and a large hood that could wrap over my matching helmet with a bit of fake fur to outline the hood.

I felt quite dashing and unique-looking, as most people rented suits and they tended to be dark blues and greens. I thought I looked perfectly the part of a skier. I even found white-rimmed goggles and a soft scarf to match.

The skis that caught my eye were bright, flashy orange, but a little too heavy and too long for me. My coach hesitated about whether they were the best fit for me, but quickly changed his mind when he saw the price tag on the skis. I didn't learn of this until later, but he apparently earned a percentage cut of the sale. No matter, despite the skis being not quite the right fit, I convinced myself I might grow into them. Even if I didn't grow in height anymore, perhaps I would become strong enough to make up for it. The store manager was a young man in his late twenties, and he smiled as I excitedly gathered all the ski gear I desired around me.

He pulled out a calculator and showed Mom the price of all the items. I watched her puff up her feathers in preparation for the bargain fight. In my head, I could hear the bells ringing as if a boxing match was about to begin. Mom was a phenomenal bargainer, always hacking and slashing away at the original price a store owner gave her. She was even able to get bargains at department stores by bullying her way to a manager if necessary. Her tongue-lashing ability not only cut us to the bone at home, but also liquefied many a shopkeeper I'd seen over the years. I only paid partial attention to her exact words. I knew she'd be talking about the quality of this or that thing to bring the price down. I watched with interest as the shopkeeper began to wilt under the pressure.

Hastily, when it looked as if Mom might give up on purchasing any of the items, the shopkeeper started piling on discounts and offers and promises. He ended up giving a hefty bundle discount for the whole lot as well as a promise to take care of me anytime I came to ski. He promised to help clean my ski gear, store my items between ski visits or while I was skiing, and if he had vouchers for free lessons, I'd get them; so on and so forth. Mom eventually felt the deal was good enough. She swiped her credit card through the machine to pay for everything, still growling at the price of it all. I tried to let her know how appreciative and grateful I was while simultaneously attempting to scoop everything up. I couldn't wait to really look at everything at home to make sure today had actually happened and all this stuff really was mine.

The very next day, I hit the slopes with my new gear. At first, I struggled for control with the slightly-too-heavy-skis. I felt that I was zooming down the slopes faster than before, which was both scary and exhilarating. I grinned to myself in the crispy coldness of the air as I rode the lift up the slope. I couldn't believe how great life was! This was happiness: the gleeful anticipation of my next run down the black diamond, the crispy wind pressing on my cheeks and eyeballs, listening to the light hum of the lift and grinding sound of skis carving against the hard snow below me.

I seldom had a seatmate as the lift took me up the hill. There was only one black diamond slope and very few people would or could go up there. Skiing wasn't exactly popular among Chinese people at the time. On my own, I would scan the slope below me as I rose. I'd plan and envision various pathways down the mountain. I could cut through the moguls here, fly over that snow mound there… It was the same slope every time, but every run felt different and so much fun!

Once the lift reached the top, I'd race down the mountain according to the rough plan I'd made on the way up. I would be flying through the snow. My leg muscles and knees burned as I pushed them to the limit so that my heavy skis would obey. Sometimes I'd be so exhausted from the run, I'd come to a stop at the bottom and find a mound of snow on the side to flop into.

Life was glorious! I had so much fun skiing that I'd sometimes catch myself laughing out loud alone.

A little past the ski lift entrance was Mr. Li, the kebab man. He was always there cooking mouth-watering beef and lamb kebabs. Mr. Li always generously coated them in whatever spices it was that made me choose his kebabs over all other food choices available every day. He would fan the delicious and irresistible aroma towards the slopes.

Periodically he'd shout in heavily regionally accented Mandarin, "Three yuan! Three yuan! Three yuan for a kebab! Ten yuan for five kebabs! Get your kebabs!", and I would. I'd buy a fistful and consume them while I sat on the lift to the top of the ski slope, then ski down and get some more if I was still hungry.

Mr. Li came to recognize my black and white checkered ski suit from afar. He'd wave or nod as I cruised to a stop in front of him and his kebabs. The kebabs steamed gloriously in the coolness of the air and he'd fan at them as he hummed to himself and brushed on the kebab sauce or sprinkled some spices.

I couldn't really chat with him, unfortunately. His accent was too heavy for me to understand much beyond the price of kebabs. I'd reach into my ski suit pocket for some crumpled cash that Mom had handed me as lunch money.

Mr. Li quickly counted out the number of kebabs I asked for, and we'd both be grinning. He was happy about the cash, and I was happier about the kebabs. Then I'd ski over to the lift and greedily wolf down the delicious spicy meat, sometimes finishing it all before I even reached the lift. Oftentimes, I did not want to waste even a minute of skiing time so a handful of kebabs were the only thing I would eat all day.

Sometimes, the workers who operated the lifts would wave at me or teasingly shout, "hey, how come you didn't get me any?" I would reply, "because they'd be cold already, and cold kebabs are no good!"

I developed the habit of waving a quick hello to Mr. Li and the lift workers each time. I imagined it must be very lonely and boring to man their stations all day.

That winter break of my senior year in high school, I woke up early most mornings so that I could get to the ski range before the slopes were too crowded. I'd sometimes be the first non-employee in the ski store, and I'd sometimes be waiting for them to open up.

I enjoyed watching the street of ski stores and businesses come to life. Everyone bustled about to get ready for that day of business, for tourists, skiers and snowboarders, families. It felt like that scene in Beauty in the Beast where Belle saunters into the town. I was definitely no "Beauty", but all the small shops opening reminded me of the movie. I wondered what my mornings would look like after I completed college. Would I be bustling about in the morning, getting ready for work just like this? I didn't even know what days would be like in college, so really, I didn't have a clue what life after college would be like at all.

Excited to start the day, I'd trudge clumsily down the street in my heavy ski boots towards the ski shop. The manager had promised Mom that I could store my ski gear for convenience. This way I didn't have to haul everything from the parking lot to the slopes each time.

At first, I insisted on struggling into all my newly purchased gear on my own. I was so over the moon with my gifted ski gear. Once I adapted to the newness, I was happy to ask the ski store employees for help with putting on my gear as they had originally offered to do when everything was purchased. I struggled with tightening some of the gear to fit just right and it made skiing uncomfortable if something was too loose or tight.

I would ski non-stop until it was time to go home, pausing only to purchase kebabs. I wasted barely a minute of my lift ticket, tirelessly going up and down the slope over and over again until sundown. I went to the ski range with such regularity that I started developing a bit of a reputation. The shopkeepers and lift workers teasingly called me "Little Snow Demon". I had already vehemently rejected the title of "Snow Princess", not wanting to be associated with being a princess at all. So, they'd give me a wink or cheeky grin when "Little Snow Demon" passed by.

3

The store manager was there every morning and every afternoon, taking care of me, helping me with my skis and engaging in some small talk. And a corner of my lonely heart craved the attention. I started opening up to him more, eventually sharing with him my cell phone number, and I learned his name, Yi. Sometimes he'd text me during the ski day if one of the veteran store members was there and interested in giving me a complimentary lesson. Before long, we began texting about things outside of just the topic of ski lessons.

We went out on our first date; I don't remember where. I think it was a pretty standard date, one where you go out and eat together, chat a bit, that sort of thing. It felt mostly just like any other time we had chatted at the ski shop, except that there was a meal, we weren't dressed in ski gear, and he wasn't assisting me in wrestling my ski boots on.

Surprisingly, I felt comfortable despite being uncomfortable with the concept of dating or romance. I thought about how useful it was to be forced to speak Mandarin only and that truly, this was a great opportunity to practice outside of talking in Chinese with Mom and Dad. My brother and I rarely spoke Mandarin to each other. Mom was busy with my brother anyways, so I talked to her seldom, and usually in English. Dad and I talked even less, since he was usually away on business and we were cautioned often about calling him due to possible long-distance rates and high cell phone bills.

Being a logical planning type, I sat down and wrote up a list of reasons to have or not to have a relationship, to decide if I should go on more dates with Yi. I knew I wanted to be in a relationship for the sake of experiencing it in a safe environment, and to fit in with my peers who were also going on dates or had been dating for a few years now. I thought about how my brother had already had his first girlfriend and kiss despite being three and a half years younger than me. I thought about how Mom and Dad often cautioned me against dating because of how a relationship would distract me from my studies and how I couldn't risk that. I thought about how my Chinese would improve from being only able to communicate with him in that language. I thought about how, since he was older and had relationship experience, he would have greater maturity and wisdom, and I might learn more from him than if I dated someone my age and the same stage I was in life.

I figured since Yi didn't attend my school, it wasn't like he could distract me during the school day once school started up again. I was confident that since this was a logical choice of a boyfriend, I wouldn't have those romantic dreamy thoughts that movie characters have that entirely distract them. In fact, when I was doing other things or skiing, I thought of him seldom and when I did, it was mostly in the context of pros and cons of choosing him as a dating experience. That was how little I knew of romance or relationships.

Yes, I eventually decided, this was a good idea. Telling him I liked him, in *that* way, wasn't hard or scary, because it wasn't actually real. I was just playing at dating. I would be able to keep my wits about me and not be driven by emotions, which made me feel safer and more in control. Dating wasn't hard. And having a boyfriend seemed nice, if for nothing else but the company and ability to share what was going on in my life.

A week after, I decided I needed to inform Mom of what I had chosen to do. I was kind of shy and Mom was originally excited to hear me share anything with her. It had been a long time since I'd confided in her, so I imagine she felt close to me again. But everything changed once she'd heard me through. And I learned very quickly how much of a mistake I had made. Mom told Dad almost immediately. They were both extremely angry that I had chosen to start dating a month before my 18th birthday, and even angrier that it was Yi.

I didn't understand why they were so emotional about it. They screamed at me that he was trash, he was nothing, a low person, commoner, low-income, not-going-anywhere type of man. They were sure he only wanted me for my body, for sex, and there was no other reason he could be dating me. They wailed that I was lowering myself and making myself just as much a piece of trash by dating him. They felt that dating at my age was far too young anyways, and the only reason I was doing so was because I must be a "slut", "whore", a "sex-crazy bitch". Their favorite saying was "sex-crazy bitch" and they used that one most often. They uttered that in enough tones and enough times to me that it's burned into my memory. Mom and Dad's primary language is Chinese, but they would make sure to vocalize the worst words and phrases in English so that you knew they were making an extra effort for you to hear their words.

"Sex-crazy bitch". "Whore". "Worthless trash".

Reeling from the shock of their vicious reaction, I didn't know what to do. I tried to explain how none of the physical stuff was appealing to me and it wasn't about that; that I'd be able to practice my Chinese and he took good care of me and my skis and so on, but none of my words could convince them that their daughter hadn't completely betrayed all their parenting by suddenly becoming the worst filth possible. All of a sudden, that logically planned out list that I had made and my beliefs of having a safety net/safe home environment to experience and experiment with having a relationship came crashing down. Not even breaking up with him would save me from that at this point; the damage was done. They made it clear who and what I was to them now.

"Sex-crazy bitch". "Whore". "Worthless trash".

4

Considering their goal was for me to not date Yi or even see him ever again, it's sad that Mom and Dad only strengthened my resolve to be with him. By calling me names and ripping my self-esteem to pieces on a daily basis, I felt greater and greater need to be with him. I felt he was the only loving one. And what was the point of breaking up with him? I was sure Mom and Dad would never love me again—or so I felt given all the things they were spewing to beat me down.

But the longer I stayed with him, the angrier they became, and more verbally and emotionally abusive. I felt my only escape was going away from everyone.

I tried my best to keep in mind that I was, after all, in my second semester of senior year. After the months in the semester and summer break, I would be going to college somewhere in the US, over 7,000 miles away. I would no longer live under their roof or see them every day. Meditating on that image of me somewhere far, far away, I felt that perhaps, I could last eight more months of this. I desperately counted down the days to freedom.

There was a better life waiting for me on the other side of the ocean. There had to be a better life there. I prayed. I just had to survive. I just had to wait. And each day, each hour, brought me closer to the greener pastures I dreamed of.

***

LISTENING TO YI'S COMPLIMENTS in Chinese was intoxicating. No one had ever made me feel so valuable, and I was drunk on the feeling of being worth something, of being attractive. These were all new thoughts and feelings and I had no defense against any of it.

Mom and Dad had complimented me growing up, but they could also flip at a moment's notice. For example, one day I could be deemed smart, other days I'd be just ok, and they'd say I could work hard to compensate for lack of naturally-born genius. Other days, I was just plain, hopelessly stupid to my parents.

Some days, I was beautiful, other days Dad might try to cut me off on my second helping at dinner, announcing that I was too fat (I was 5'4 and 120lb). Occasionally, Mom would yank me out of my desk chair while I was at my computer. She believed that sitting in a chair caused my butt to be offensively large. She was disgusted by the sight of me in jeans, and insisted I should wear long skirts or dresses to hide the unsightliness of my body. It was impossible to believe their compliments, because they could change their opinion so quickly. It was easier to believe in their criticisms and insults. I tried to just filter it all out, believing nothing that they said about me.

My senior year final semester was torture. My normal day was to: wake up, get yelled at by mom. She'd follow me down to breakfast and continue to rail while I ate. I'd sling on my heavy backpack and head to school.

At school, things would be peaceful. After all my school activities, I'd come home. The moment I entered the front door, the yelling would begin again. I would trudge upstairs to my room and unpack my bag while being yelled at some more until about an hour before dinner. Mom would go and rest her voice and I'd enjoy the silence for a little while and get some homework done. Dad would arrive home right around 6pm, he'd yell at me some more, curse me, or glare at me over dinner, then he would take a break to watch the evening news.

I would finish eating in mostly silence, trudge upstairs to my room and close the door while I finished my homework. Closing any door was pointless though, Mom and Dad had removed locks from doors for years. Not even the bathroom door had a lock on it, just so Mom and Dad could open a door at any time. Only their room had locks, and even then, it was only the door to the bathroom. I would be sitting in my chair with my textbooks open and Mom would storm up the stairs to scream how worthless and stupid I was.

Eventually, Mom would tire of beating me with words, so she would leave. Dad would rally and continue the tirade, until he felt it was bedtime. One last hate-filled glare and I'd be allowed to turn the lights out and go to sleep, to start the next day.

My school used the International Baccalaureate (IB) program for high school academics. All the exams were two-year cumulative content and I had six of those to take in a few months. People in the IB program were normally expected to take three higher level and three standard level courses. For those who were driven or had parents driving them, the principal made certain exceptions. A selection of students could apply to take four higher level and two standard level courses instead. I was among the students that successfully applied for this exception.

By necessity, we buried ourselves in coursework. So, I studied every day. I took higher level Biology, English, Economics, and Chinese. Chinese was particularly challenging. The class was developed for native speakers of Chinese and I was not a native speaker or at the level of a native speaker. I did my best, but sometimes became very frustrated at how effortless homework or tests could be for actual native speakers in the class. That mainly stemmed from my jealousy. I wished that I could be as good. I strived to be among the highest performing students for Chinese and all other classes.

IB exams were out of seven points and to earn a seven you had to score in the top 7% of all the kids taking the exam that year from all over the world. I knew I was going to a US college and some US colleges weren't accepting IB courses as credits at all, or would only take 6's and 7's for credit. If the stress of school wasn't enough to cause me suicidal thoughts, Mom and Dad's incessant tirade most definitely was.

"Sex-crazy bitch". "Whore". "Worthless trash". When these were worn down from overuse, they threw in "piece of shit" and other synonyms. Other times, I was "fat", "lazy", "stupid", "ugly", "worst daughter in the world", "waste of life/time/money/effort raising me", "should never have been born". All to get me to do what they wanted me to do or be what they wanted me to be.

Consciously or unconsciously, they felt that if they called me those names enough times, the outcome they wanted would happen. In their minds, I would change and no longer be those things if they hurt me and shamed me enough. It had worked in the past when I was younger. But I was about eighteen now and about to be a college student. While their verbal abuse was effective for venting their emotions, it didn't always yield their desired results. However, that didn't stop them from trying harder. They just continued ramping up in creativity, intensity, and frequency of verbal abuse that year.

There are words that have stayed with me even after not living at home or hearing them call me that anymore. I guess it really sank in. Frequently, without their prompting, I've put myself down because they had done so for so long. I actively work at silencing their voices from my past. It's not easy.

* * *

ONE TIME, MOM CAME INTO MY ROOM with a box while I was studying for my IB exams. I had never seen a condom before she started casting them like frisbees at my face. Maybe she was aiming at the textbooks I had spread out in front of me. Or maybe she didn't particularly care and just wanted to chuck them in my general direction. Some of them hit me, cool plastic rebounding off my face from the force of her flinging them.

I sat motionless while my open textbook became covered in condoms. Arguing with my parents made them angry and sometimes led to me crying. Crying just made things worse. They'd point out how ugly my cry-face was, make fun of my nose dripping, or sneer at me for being such a weakling and unable to control my emotions.

Being passive and quiet made them angry because I wasn't reacting, but it seemed to be my best option. So, I sat there patiently until she became tired and left the room before I cleared the condoms to the side of my desk. I didn't have time to process everything they said or did anymore, as exams drew closer. So, I continued to study from my textbook with a small mound of condoms on the side.

The next day, Dad came in with a box. Instead of throwing the condoms at me though, he set them on my desk. I noticed that he had bought a larger box than Mom had, and a foreign brand as opposed to the local Chinese brand condoms Mom had purchased. I hid a tiny smile from him as he stormed away and shut the door. It was just like Dad to buy the more expensive thing, and just like Mom to go for the cheaper ones. I took the box and placed it in the same drawer where I had scooped up all the condoms Mom had given me, and pushed the drawer closed.

At this time, I hadn't talked to Yi about sex yet, nor was I even interested. I barely tolerated kissing, and I absolutely hated anything with tongue. It made me think of alien horror or zombie horror movies and just made me sick.

* * *

During this time, Mom and Dad tried various approaches; Mom's being the most creative of the two of them. Sometimes she'd go beyond using her insults. She made me go for multiple pap smears and blood tests that semester. I wasn't sure if this was because they were convinced they would find something which they could use to further hurt and shame me, or if it was just to use the tests as a weird form of punishment.

One time, she claimed that having sex seriously lowered one's immune system, making it so that I would get sick, and sick people in her mind were despicable. Mom's philosophy was that getting sick was one of the worst things, because not only did the sick person feel bad, but also it made them a burden on others. Being a burden was selfish and unforgivable.

She often had preached throughout my childhood how much she hated people who were burdens, glaring at us children significantly, so we'd better make ourselves useful. Mom loudly shared her opinion on how repugnant the act of sex was. Sex was wrong for me and distasteful. Pleasure-seeking was for dirty perverts and shameless whores. She believed that it was a married woman's duty so she allowed for it to happen from time to time. She explained to me her beliefs many times.

Sometimes, I wonder how Mom and Dad had managed to have kids since each time she talked about sex, it was quite clear she despised it. Unwittingly, her ranting further cemented in the idea for me that not everyone desires sex but it has to happen with your partner.

Dad tried making physical threats to Yi's safety through terrorizing me. Dad threatened me that if I continued to date Yi, he would call the police to round Yi up on some bogus charge or hire some thugs to beat Yi to pulp. Dad thought I'd fear for Yi's safety or that I'd at the very least pass the message on. And I did. I was confiding in Yi for just about everything at that time. Yi scoffed at the idea of thugs, but was worried about the police, since he did actually have a prior conviction. He briefly described the details of his charge.

There was a fight a few years ago where he was outnumbered, but he successfully defended himself and fought them off. He was charged for physical assault, since the judge had listened to the multiple voices of the people who he fought as opposed to his lone voice. It didn't help that he had beaten one of them so badly that there was a hefty medical bill. The judge said that the force Yi had used was excessive, even for self-defense. At least that's what Yi told me. I guess this story should have scared me, but I didn't view myself as one of the men who would attack him, and I didn't think he'd do that to a woman, and me in particular.

Each day Mom and Dad hurt me, but I felt that I couldn't focus on the negativity of it all or let any of Mom and Dad's words get under my skin. I was afraid I'd fall apart.

After the first rape, even though the sexual experiences were painful and unwanted, I viewed it as a necessary trade, so that I could cry on Yi's shoulder. The pain I suffered under his hands and under his body hurt much less than listening to Mom and Dad, especially since I needed him for survival, or so I felt. Each day brought me closer to that plane ride across the ocean. I held on.

I continued to perform in school, continued to perform in my extracurriculars, using education as my coping mechanism. I sang in the honor choir, and even performed for the final time in the annual High School Talent Show. I never won, but I learned something new and put on one act each year.

One year I sang and played the piano. One year I learned and performed a traditional Chinese song and dance. This year, I had learned Latin dance with some friends and created some choreography.

At school, I hung out with my friends. People complimented me on my productivity and seeming zest for life. Everything seemed fantastic on the surface. I don't think anyone would have imagined how my life actually was. I prayed desperately for September to arrive sooner. I promised myself I would fly away from this life or I would kill myself to escape. And that made life livable. There would be an end, one way or another.

5

Mom and Dad's parenting methods had me on my toes most of the time. I remember the first report card I received from Kindergarten.

I remember my small backpack bouncing with me as I ran down the sidewalk to mom. I was so happy, because I had scored so well on everything. It was a happiness so pure and my childlike voice was high-pitched and animated as I babbled to her about my day and pulled out the piece of paper. I didn't know about different paper weights or that that was called a heavier weight of paper, but I could feel the slightly thicker, slightly heavier paper in my hand and I appreciated the novelty of it. I didn't put it in my backpack after the teacher had given it to me, for fear that it might become crinkled in my bag. So, I clenched it in my little hands and waved it in the air, feeling the wind fluttering against it as I ran.

But Mom was not excited; her face was stern as she scanned my report card. Then she asked me, "Were you the best in your class?"

I was confused. I stammered that I only knew what my table mates had on their report cards, because we had looked at each other's. We compared the sticker smiley faces that had been pressed onto our pieces of paper.

Then Mom asked how I had done relative to my table and I mumbled that I had the best scores out of my table, but that was only three other kids. Impatiently, she waved off my response. She sighed— it didn't matter if I was the best of my class even, was I the best in the grade? And even then, what about other schools in the city? What about all the other schools in the country? I couldn't even begin to think how many kids and how many report cards I was expected to compete against. But before I could start processing that, she vocalized to me what she really wanted me to remember.

"You will never be the best one, so you have to keep working."

And I felt my happy smile fade away. She was Mom and she was right. She explained that the world was so vast and there were so many people, so many more people than I could even fathom. I felt I needed to be the best one so that Mom would be happy with me, but I would never be the best— how could I be? How could that be determined? How could I show Mom that I was the best one? How could I make her love my report card as I had? Suddenly, my report card was nothing. I needed to work so much harder. I should never have been satisfied by smiley face stickers and a couple high marks on a piece of paper. I was wrong.

I felt so bewildered. I didn't know what to think or feel. In my confusion, Mom informed me that in future, she would let me know when I could be happy about something. And this wasn't one of those times. So, I left my report card in her hands, and I went to my room to think about what she said. In later years, even if a report card was all A's, I merely mumbled it to her matter-of-factly. I felt no pride or joy in it. It was just an expectation. I had met the standard, which meant I was doing my job. Anything less than that was just not doing my job. There was nothing to be proud of or happy about unless Mom said so. Mom's goal had been for me to never be complacent with my academic performance, but as part of her method, I also never learned to be satisfied with my achievements.

* * *

PERHAPS SHE FELT SHE had been too harsh in her lecture. Later on, she encouraged Dad to be more encouraging to the kids alongside her. This forced positivity was unnatural for them. It was easier for them to criticize and scold. As a result, if my academic performance pleased them, they would suddenly go from cursing my existence to bizarrely singing my praises and boasting to friends and relatives, buying treats and toys to reward me. Their treatment could fluctuate wildly—each week different from the next, sometimes changing day to day or even within a few hours.

Sometimes, rewards were lavish, such as the expensive ski gear. The total cost of all the equipment purchased for me that day was more than the average Chinese person's month of wages. And they never let me forget it. My brother was better at taking advantage of these "good times"; his room slowly filled up with multiple laptops, sound systems, different kinds of guitars, a drum set in the basement, and whatever else caught his fancy.

I hated when "bad times" came around and Mom and Dad used the gifts from "good times" to guilt trip me; to call me ungrateful or unworthy of those previous gifts because of how I'd disappointed them by being such a failure. "I can't believe I bought ____ for you. You are a waste of money", they would say. Things that they bought me that made me happy were used to make me feel like trash. I still regard gifts suspiciously, fearing they will be weaponized against me at any moment.

Even into my late teens and adult years, Mom would sometimes bring up shoes she bought for me when I was a toddler. She would expound on how funds were extremely tight back then and toddler me was growing up so fast that she knew I would outgrow those shoes rapidly. She debated forever to justify the cost of it. And here was the toddler grown past that stage, showing how all the effort she put into raising me had resulted in the waste of space that I had become because of whatever I had done in that moment that pissed her off.

* * *

WE ALL HAD JOBS IN THE FAMILY. Myself and my brother's jobs were to be the best students ever. Mom's job was to do the lion's share of parenting and all of the house care. Dad's was to make money to support the family and occasionally participate as a parent.

Dad was an executive manager at an energy company (which meant very little and sounded very boring to me as a child). He worked both away from home and at home. In my memory, I don't recall him taking a sick day. Most times, his work schedule was rigid like the one he kept at home. Unless he was travelling, or there was some rare special thing going on at work, he left and returned at the same time each work day.

Dad was so out of the baby care-taking picture, that to make light of his absence, Mom's favorite story was about when Dad nearly killed me when I was just one month old. Dad would chuckle guiltily, but would not deny anything during Mom's telling. She details that after giving birth to me, she had taken over all the necessary tasks to keep a baby alive and thriving. She fed me, she burped me, she rocked me, she dressed me, she wiped me, she spent all her waking and what precious little sleeping moments she had with me. Dad was still working on his PhD, and she felt she needed to take care of all the baby work so that he could continue pursuing his degree, since I had already destroyed hers. But after one month of her seemingly thankless caring of me, she had enough. She lost her temper partly from going crazy with lack of sleep and yelled at Dad about how he didn't care about me. She screamed about how she was doing everything and he wasn't doing a damn thing for this baby that was also his. She stated she was going out and leaving, and Dad yelled back that he could take care of it, since taking care of a baby was easy. He snarled at her to go out and away, determined to show her just how easy baby care was. Since Mom desperately needed a break and wanted to teach Dad a lesson about how hard her job was, she snatched up the car keys and stormed out of the rundown apartment that they were renting at the time.

They lived paycheck to paycheck and pinched pennies like crazy in order to pay. Since Mom had stormed out late at night, she really had nowhere to go except the 24/7 supermarket. So, she drove and parked at the grocery store, angrily marching up the grocery aisles, shoving a hapless, empty grocery cart in front of her. I'm not sure how long she was gone, but eventually, she had worked off enough steam, returned the cart, and drove home.

I had been crying when she left, but when she opened the door to the apartment, she saw me lying there on the floor, quiet, wide-eyed, staring at her and blinking slowly. Dad noticed Mom's entry and pointed at my now quiet form, "See? I know how to take care of a baby. She isn't even crying anymore".

Mom came over to me and picked me up, noticing my quietness, but also noticing my round belly. My belly was too round, even by baby standards. I hadn't been a large baby, barely six pounds, and at one month old, I was still a tiny thing.

Mom describes how she picked me up gently and began to stroke my distended belly. As she rubbed, I began to throw up milk, and then more milk, and then more milk. Being a newborn, I only needed a small number of ounces of milk. However, each time I had cried, Dad had forced the milk bottle into my mouth and fed me until I was so full, I could barely breathe, let alone cry anymore. My face was tight and red from discomfort of being overfed and the desire to cry.

From then on, this increased Mom's resolve of being the caregiver, since she didn't trust him to know what to do with a baby. Much of the parenting process as we grew up went similarly.

6

Dad was and is an extremely driven man. His upbringing was not easy. Born in a poor family, his parents were assembly line factory workers that barely made enough to provide for the family of three kids. Dad was the eldest child and the only son, which meant that his parents put most of their hope for the future in him, ingraining in him the need to provide and support the family when he became able to do so. He told me stories of how, when the family only could afford to buy one egg that week, he would be the one to eat the egg. My grandma hand-made most of the family's clothing and shoes to save money for food and other necessities when they were growing up.

In his teenage years, the Cultural Revolution happened and all schools were shut down since Chairman Mao felt that an education and experience in agriculture was more important than school learning. Able-bodied teenagers of a certain age range were sent to work in the fields and Dad was one of them. For a while, he was a rice farmer.

Although I am not sure how long he lived away from his own family to work in the fields as a rice farmer, I do know that he never attended middle and high school. When the government shifted its views and strategies towards educating people and opening schools again, Dad self-studied to be accepted and graduate from a college in China, later accepting an opportunity to get a Ph.D. from Northwestern University in America. I was conceived and born during his time at Northwestern.

When he first started working, he worked for very low wages in a lab, later getting into the oil and gas business with his Ph.D. in petroleum engineering. This job made more money, but he found other opportunities that let him not only use his engineering degree, but also his bilingual abilities. As his career took off, he began going on more and more business trips, which meant Mom would be alone in taking of us children.

One time, Dad went away to Hong Kong for six months on an extended business trip. This was quite a long time to leave Mom alone in America, across the ocean, to take care of myself and my younger brother. I couldn't have been more than six years old, which would make my brother two or three.

Mom was terrified of something bad happening. Dad had been working several years now, and they had saved up to buy a house, but I don't know if it was in a safe neighborhood. At the very least, Mom didn't fully trust enough to not have some security arrangements so that we could sleep soundly at night.

At night, Mom would bring us all to the master bedroom. She would keep a baseball bat under the bed within easy reach in case she had to defend us from an intruder. She would also set up the house alarm and motion-sensor on the first floor.

One time, I felt hungry at night and I got up quietly, careful not to wake Mom or my brother. I snuck downstairs to get some bread that was out on the counter, but doing so set off the motion detector. The alarm went off, the sound of the siren rebounding off the walls. I panicked and crawled behind the living room sofa.

Upstairs, Mom blindly grasped in the dark for the bat when she realized that I was not in bed. She began screaming my name and throwing on all the light switches, but over the sound of the alarm, I was too afraid to answer.

She found me crying behind the sofa and then chuckled with relief when she saw the bag of bread I was still clutching in my hand. Mom shut off the alarm, but it had already automatically called the police. The police were scary, too, but she brought me over and explained to police what had happened.

Dad bought a door jammer and Mom began using that to barricade us in at night. It was a long metal stick that pushed against the door knob and the floor, making it near impossible to open the door from the other side.

I don't really remember what it was like not having dad around, but I do remember the barricaded door at night and mom's fear. She would have us two kids sleep on either side of her, a mother cub protecting her baby cubs.

7

The story of how Mom and Dad met each other and got married is rather uninspiring. They both were born to poor families and studied harder than their peers. The highest scoring students all over China would be assigned to Beijing, the capital. Mom and Dad scored #1 for their respective provinces, and so they went to the capital. China has had this kind of a tradition for centuries. Always the ones who did best in the national tests were sent to the capital to work.

Mom was nine years younger than Dad, which meant that he had already been there a while. On top of being impressive enough to be sent to the capital, they were also considered to be top performers in their individual work locations. When the government started a program to teach English to Chinese people so that they could work internationally or with foreign companies, their individual supervisors both separately recommended Mom and Dad to be sent to this program.

This program for elites is where Mom and Dad met. They both did stunningly. During this time, it was common for friends, family, and acquaintances to make recommendations or suggestions for matchmaking. Mom had a friend who was not yet married and Dad was aging past the optimal marrying age for men (late 20s at that time). Since Mom greatly respected and admired Dad and she had a friend closer to

Dad's age who also was unmarried, she reached out to him to set up a date for the two of them.

Dad readily agreed, beginning to feel some pressure for marriage and being quite romantically inexperienced and awkward. He had been so focused on his studies, working, and taking care of his family, that he had actually not experienced romance at all. Mom has stories of ex-boyfriends but Dad has just one story of a failed match that one of his professors tried to set up before he met Mom.

The day of the date, Mom waited with Dad at the agreed upon location to meet. The idea was for her friend to meet them there and then Dad and her friend would go off to have a meal or something. Mom and Dad being very responsible and serious, had both arrived slightly early and chatted idly while waiting for Mom's friend. As the minutes stretched on, it became obvious that her friend had flaked or at the very least was going to be embarrassingly late.

Mom felt terribly guilty for wasting Dad's time and energy, so as an apology she went on a date with him so that his trip wouldn't for nothing. Dad again readily agreed, and he invited Mom over for a meal. At this time, Dad still knew how to cook and was a good cook, while Mom was very young and new to adulting. She was actually very inexperienced in cooking. On top of his performance in the English class, Dad's cooking also impressed Mom.

Dad was a very functional man. The apartment had no decorations, just piles and piles of the books that he studied with machine-like determination. He had a glass top coffee table with numerous newspaper clippings carefully arranged under the glass.

While Dad cooked, Mom skimmed over some of the newspaper clippings. Most of them were Confucian-inspired life wisdoms on how to be a good person while others were related to diet and health. When she asked Dad where they were from, he proudly talked about how his dad always cut out and sent him these newspaper clippings.

Mom had a far-off look as she imagined what that must have been like; my grandfather reading each newspaper and then getting out his scissors to carefully cut out the stories then mail them to Dad in the post. Imagining Dad opening the letter, reading each clip, and then carefully adding them under the coffee table glass top. She dreamily confided that that's part of what really won her over. She loved that he was so studious, so smart, so loyal, and loving to his parents.

They dated some more, and Dad saved up his money to buy Mom a fancy coat, but he didn't have much and such a purchase was very expensive for him. She cherished the coat greatly. I don't know what it looked like, they were too poor to take pictures.

Shortly after this date, Dad was accepted into Northwestern's PhD program. He couldn't afford to bring Mom along with, but he was going to be leaving within months. His proposal to mom went something along the lines of "You are smart, and I am smart; you are beautiful and I am handsome. Together, we will be a great team and have amazing babies. Will you be my wife?" Mom agreed.

Not having the funds to afford a wedding, they instead put on their best clothes and Dad rode his bike, the only form of transportation he owned. Mom perched on the back of the bicycle on their way to the courthouse to apply for the legal documentation. To celebrate the wedding, Dad rode with Mom around Tiananmen Square.

I imagine them smiling and giggling on a basic and scuffed up old Chinese bicycle as they ride around the large square; but they weren't in love, or at least Dad wasn't. Dad, at this time, said that since they didn't have enough time to really date and fall in love, they would instead have "love after marriage". With what disposable income Dad had at the time, he was able to afford to have one marriage photo taken. Mom has preserved that photo in our family album. They never had a wedding ceremony.

* * *

WHEN DAD LEFT FOR THE US after only being married to Mom for a month, it was a big shift in Mom's life. Although I've always seen her as very independent and capable, she describes this period of her life as falling apart. She was working hard, but at the time—with the technology they had available to them and the high cost of communicating overseas—it was very challenging to keep up the relationship. Long distance calls sounded like they were talking from opposite sides of a tunnel, hardly intimate or romantic. They were only able to afford one international phone call a month and usually wrote letters. Dad was terrible at writing letters, so Mom was more often the only one sending them. Despite what Dad had said, Mom was definitely already in love with him and missed him terribly. Mom's friends were concerned about her emotional and physical health and tried their best to comfort her.

When Dad finally saved enough money through working while being in school for his PhD, Mom applied and was accepted to University of Chicago. Full of nerves and excitement, Mom packed for America. It was her first time leaving the country, but more than her first experiences and thoughts about America, she was fixated on reuniting with Dad. Neither Mom and Dad are verbally or physically lovey-dovey, but it was these moments where I could clearly see, love was there.

She expected to see him as he had always been, wiry and thin—they had even been able to fit in the same pants at one point. But after two years of being in the US, being too busy to cook, he had eaten a decent amount of fast food at this point, and had gained a lot of weight. To Mom's disappointment and distress, he was much flabbier than before.

He had also picked up a crassness and roughness to his speech that actually had her in tears over how vulgar his language had become. He swore a lot and although it was not directed at her, it still really upset her sensibilities. She finally yelled at him about it and he gradually broke the habit.

Starting school, things were a struggle, not only because English was Mom's second language, but also because the US life and school system were so different from China. To make matters worse, there was a lot of financial pressure. Without a significant grant or financial aid of some form, they would not be able to afford both Mom and Dad being in school simultaneously for long. And then Mom became pregnant.

She continued to go to classes up until her belly became too large for her to do so. She felt very conspicuous and very ashamed, especially when her belly became too large for her to hide. She could feel the judging eyes of other students on her.

That's when her old life ended, in her words. And a new life began. A life of slavery where her life revolved around caring for Dad and us kids, like the earth around the sun, helpless and bound.

8

Dad was extremely regimented and ran our family similarly. Breakfast, lunch, and dinner were always at the same time: 7am, noon, and 6pm. If you showed up to any of these meals late or if the family was not a complete unit at the table, both parents would be cross but Dad especially, would become very irritated.

Dad had a big voice, so he'd bellow at whoever was missing with increasing anger, volume, and frequency. Mom took some voice lessons over the years to improve her volume, but in the years prior to her being satisfied with how loud she could shout, she bought a Chinese bell. It was a miniature version of a traditional Chinese bronze bell similar to the ones you saw in Chinese temples. It had a very clear, lingering tone when struck.

Mom would strike it according to her mood and expectations, sometimes pounding away at the poor bell when she was enraged. When I think about it, my ears still ring painfully.

This sentiment about time and scheduled events applied to vacations as well. I remember one time we went on a family vacation to the beach. Dad typically had a detailed itinerary of what time we would be doing what where, even including travelling time. When we were too small, these were not shared with us kids, but as we grew older, he would typically print out and hand copies to us. He would even have them stapled and neatly put in protective plastic sleeves so that they wouldn't be crinkled.

On his itinerary, most hours of the day would be blocked out back to back with various events he had planned or reservations he had made. This meant that if something was a hold up—typically us kids—he would fly into a rage and yell he didn't want us kids anymore. If Mom had something to do with the delay, which was rare, he would even go so far as to bellow he didn't want the whole family anymore. In the privacy of the hotel room, he'd holler that we were all burdens.

The goal for 365 days of the year was to avoid being called a burden or a "piece of shit". By Mom and Dad's standards, it was frighteningly easy to be a "piece of shit". Any minute of any given day you could become a "piece of shit". If you woke up later than a certain hour, went to bed later than a certain hour, had less productive hours in a day than a certain amount; if you sat a certain way, dressed a certain way, slept a certain way, talked a certain way, treated them or spoke to them a certain way, got a bad grade even if it was your best effort, you were still a "piece of shit" . If a task wasn't completed in a certain time frame, you would also be a "piece of shit".

Yet, somehow, I survived by learning their system and doing my best to navigate it. Sometimes, I had to be a "piece of shit" in some lesser categories, balancing the greater "piece of shit" and the lesser "piece of shit" status. For example, since I knew that Mom and Dad valued an A in Math more than an A in English, I would prioritize if I couldn't achieve A's in both classes. On days where they were in a good mood or you magically produced all the results that they wanted, the world was full of rainbows and butterflies.

Since my status in the family could go from extremely loved to extremely hated seemingly at the drop of a hat, I learned to process things differently so as not to be constantly depressed. Getting work done or fulfilling their requests was a matter of avoiding being called a "piece of shit". Being called "piece of shit" became the way to make me do things. Mom and Dad would follow me around the house calling me "piece of shit" until I did their bidding. I carried this into my adulthood, often calling myself a "piece of shit" if I felt I hadn't gotten enough done in a day just as Mom and Dad had always done.

One of the issues linked to constantly using shit-talk to motivate myself was that my self-image or self-esteem was often quite low. Sometimes, it was so low that shit-talk stopped working. I would give up and accept that I was just a "piece of shit" and that it was hopeless. Mom and Dad were right, I was a "piece of shit", I'd always be a "piece of shit", and what was the point of fighting my "piece-of-shit-ness" or trying to satisfy them since I was only ever going to be a "piece of shit"?

Other downsides to shit-talk meant that sometimes, I wouldn't or couldn't understand why someone would be friends with me unless I could prove to myself that I was of some functional use in another person's life. Oftentimes, it didn't occur to me to be a friend or to make friends. I matter-of-factly accepted that I was a "piece of shit" and why would anyone want to be friends with a "piece of shit".

Even if it weren't for my own self-esteem issues, Mom and Dad made it very challenging to have any friends growing up. If they met any of my classmates, Mom and Dad would inevitably determine that the kid was a "piece of shit" by their standards and I shouldn't associate with "piece of shit" people. Sometimes they would get very specific and like bullies, make fun of if my classmate had a large forehead or ears or something. Although these comments were made in the privacy of our home, I always felt bad for the kid they were criticizing but I never knew what to say.

Furthermore, Dad would emphasize how we would be moving shortly, since we moved every couple of years, and that I would never see my classmates again, so I shouldn't form any deep friendships. He felt that all friendships in elementary, middle, and high school were pointless and explained this to me often. He himself did not have any significant friendships in these years of his life, so naturally, he felt the same about mine.

9

Making friends may not have been at the top of Mom and Dad's list of priorities, but they did feel that it was very important for me and my brother to see more of the world and more of China.

Mom and Dad really love their country, and this was instilled in me as well. We traveled all over, as far west as Gobi Desert and the Tibetan plateau and as far east as the ocean. Travelling was an eye-opening experience. We ate lots of different foods, listened to other languages and dialects, and saw a little of how other people lived their lives.

One time, we visited Dalian, a coastal city, known for its abundance of fresh seafood. There was a park next to the ocean, full of little rides and local eats. Usually, I was the thrill seeker, the one who wanted to ride all the rides, especially the bigger ones. My brother and Mom had no interest in such things, and rather preferred to observe. So, Dad kept me company on any crazy rides I wanted to try.

This amusement park had a bungee tower. You would awkwardly teeter out onto the jumping plank with your legs bound together and spring over the ocean. I watched someone fall in the distance, bounce up and down with the bungee rope, and dangle patiently while a small motorboat puttered over to release the jumper and bring them back to land. There was something amazing about that. Ecstatically, I pointed and announced, "I want to do that".

Dad balked this time, but he bought me a ticket, and the family rode the elevator up with me to the top of the tower. Mom was always afraid of heights, so this was very uncomfortable for her. I could see her turning pale, but she was determined to catch everything on camera.

The tower staff wrapped my lower legs in their bungee contraption and attached the rope. With my legs wrapped together, I needed help to get in position on the plank. I hobbled awkwardly along as two guys dragged me over. They instructed me to raise my arms and pose for the camera, which I did. Then it was time to go. I tipped over the edge…and then I was flying.

I'd never experienced this level of adrenaline rush. My bloodstream was super charged with happiness. No sound, image, language, dance, nothing could express the ecstasy of this moment! I forgot even that there was a bungee cord and I couldn't care less. I was flying. I was free. Free to dive and fly and I was intoxicated beyond thought. I wanted to drink it all in and keep it forever.

Flying.

Flying.

Flying.

It was so brief. The bungee cord reached its maximum length at the end of my dive, and I reached towards the blue ocean waters below me. Then I was bouncing, the cord twanging me up and down, viewing sea, then sky, then sea, then sky, until finally, I hung upside down over the water, spinning slowly. I felt my heart drop with the emptiness of having been so filled with this intensity of emotion for the first time in my life.

The motorboat picked me up and took me back to shore. I couldn't forget that brief moment. I wanted to hold onto that moment and die in that moment to make it last forever. My heart ached.

At the end of that vacation, when we went back home, I looked at all the tall buildings we drove by and fantasized jumping off of all of them.

10

Other than wanting us children to be absolute ace students, Mom especially wanted us to be in control of our emotions. She hated when someone lost control of their emotions or cried. She felt it was embarrassing and shameful and was the trait of weak and horrid people.

Roughly once a year, we went to Shanghai to celebrate the Chinese New Year holidays with Dad's side of the family. One time when I was around 12, my older cousin was really crying and sobbing about something. All the relatives had gathered to meet at my grandparents' apartment and we were supposed to go eat some nice dinner together that Dad had a reservation for, but my cousin just cried and cried. I was several years younger than her and too distant to know or understand what was upsetting her. My auntie whispered that my cousin had a broken heart from a recent breakup, and I nodded knowingly in answer, but I had no idea what that meant.

Normally, in the power dynamic of the traditional Chinese family, it would be awkward or inappropriate for someone who had married into the family to do something about this situation. However, Dad—being the first and only son in his family meant that Mom's status was greatly elevated as a result. Although not directly blood related, she could stride into a room and order about my aunts, Dad's sisters. She rarely exercised this power, but this time she did.

At first, Mom and Dad murmured sympathetic things, but delays always irritated them. My cousin sat on the bed in the bedroom and continued to cry. My aunts softly petted her shoulders trying to comfort her.

When it became clear that my cousin's sobbing was going to make us all late for the dinner reservation, Mom stood up decisively. She herded everyone out of the bedroom in which my cousin was sobbing, and flung the door shut with my cousin alone inside. The door closed with a such a loud bang that shocked us all so much that everyone jumped and stopped speaking or moving.

Mom spoke loudly so that my cousin could hear through the door and explained to the room of astounded relatives that when my cousin stopped crying, she could leave the room, and not before. She derisively wrinkled her nose and announced "no one can cry forever".

Mom held tightly onto the door knob, her knuckles white as she held the door strongly shut. No one went to contest her grip. My cousin shortly after quietened and mumbled thickly through the door if she could please be let out. Her eyes were red and her face was streaky, but she was obedient now and had stopped crying. After glaring at my cousin to make sure she wasn't going to be weak anymore, Mom determined we could all go to dinner.

I became more terrified of crying in front of Mom and Dad after that incident. In Chinese, there is an old idiom that goes 杀鸡给猴看 (sha ji gei hou kan) which literally means to kill a chicken in front of a monkey. It meant that the chicken was an example and by being slaughtered in front of the monkey, the monkey would see the example, be frightened, and obey so as to avoid a similar fate. And I was the monkey.

Another lesson was "it doesn't matter how shitty of a situation you are in, this is the one you are in, and especially if you can't get out of it, there's no sense in complaining; make it work, learn to survive".

Mom and Dad may not have been like other parents. They treated me unlike how other parents treated their kids. But that didn't matter. It was interesting to know how other parents parented and treated their kids, but largely irrelevant. This was the life I was in, and I could not have other parents, so I had better make the best of what I had.

One year in school, our teacher encouraged us to write diary entries. She felt it would help us get better grades in English and that it was a great habit to have. Wanting to please her and Mom and Dad and get the best grades I could, I complied with fervor. This began my diary writing habit, which actually continued throughout my life.

Some of my diary entries were filled with child-like excitement and babble about various adventures of the day, but some took on a much darker note.

The first memory I have of writing that I hated Mom and Dad was in early middle school. I couldn't articulate the reason I had hatred for them well. It confused me that I did have hatred for them because they had instructed me over and over that kids love their parents and parents love them back. This was taught to me as if a law of physics.

And yet, I wrote in my diary that I wanted them dead. I felt terrible for having this desire, and tried my best to bury it.

In second grade, I met a teacher; I forget her name. She usually taught eighth graders, but for whatever reason, for that one school year she wanted to teach second grade. I loved her. I loved her so much and I don't remember why.

At a spelling bee after spelling a word correctly, I sought her face in the crowd first. I looked for her smile, and it lit me up always. Unconsciously, I chose her to be my make-believe mother that year, starting a pattern that I continued all through to the end of high school. After having such an amazing "mom" that year, I thought to myself, why not continue to do so? If I could not have the Mom and Dad I wanted at home, I could play pretend at school.

In the following years of school, I would pick out one male teacher and one female teacher to be Mom and Dad of the year. Oftentimes, my homeroom teacher would be one of my pretend parents.

Some students accused me of trying to be or actually being the teacher's pet. It's true that I would give my pretend parents handmade little gifts or cards sometimes, or stay after class to chit chat with them about my day. In high school, one teacher commented that this was a bit odd, but I couldn't explain to her why I did what I did.

11

Mom and Dad believed strongly in education. Tutoring costs in Beijing were very low. You could get a tutor in most subjects for $10 an hour or less in those days. They would commute to your home and not charge you for it. Besides, Dad was paid US wages for living in China.

So, right from the get-go, before we had even moved into a home, we were already receiving tutoring. When we first arrived, the company put us in a hotel, so Mom and Dad set us kids up with swimming lessons at the hotel pool.

Prior to this I'd had the standard kid's swimming lessons at the community pool, learning how to duck my head under the water without panicking, and doggie paddling in the shallow side of the pool.

This swimming tutor actually happened to be a Beijing Olympic team talent recruiter who also coached swimming in his free time. Mom and Dad mentioned several years later that he had actually asked if he could recruit me for the Beijing Olympic swimming team. He felt that I could be a great swimmer, because at that age, I showed signs that I might grow into an ideal "swimmer's body". Relative to other Chinese girls, I already was much taller, with longer arms and legs.

Many children recruited as Olympic hopefuls come from poor families. Their families are paid hefty sums, and enjoy the status that comes with having an Olympic-hopeful child. Mom and Dad declined, not needing the money and knowing that the Olympic training was brutal. Besides, they believed education—not sports—was my ticket to the "good life". Still, it's interesting to daydream about it sometimes, how different a life path that would have and could have been. I wonder how far I would have gone.

I took all sorts of classes under mom's selected roster of tutors. Some things I only gained a rudimentary understanding of, while I continued to work on others over time. I learned everything including belly dancing, singing, math, oil painting, piano, and Chinese.

I often felt that school was much easier than being at home, especially over longer holidays. Tutors always focused on just me because there were no other students. At school, the teacher could call on other students and assignments were generally easier. I could get away with zoning out sometimes if I was exhausted.

Since my learning curve was above average, my tutors generally took a great liking to me and would sometimes try to sneak in an extra 15-30 minutes of tutoring at no extra financial cost. My learning curve I attributed not to intelligence, since Mom and Dad had assured me I had only slightly above average intelligence. Instead, I believe it is due to constantly taking classes in new things, training my brain to take in new information. Although I appreciated and loved most of my tutors and their extra teaching time, this also meant more work for me. Focusing on the positive, this was several years of amazing growth for me. I kept learning and learning.

Not surprisingly, from Mom and Dad's conditioning and just from being the kid that I was, I wanted to please. I wanted my tutors to like me and be impressed by my progress. I wanted to feel special and bright, despite not being naturally "gifted".

I would try my best to be the best student possible to my tutors. My tutors loved how driven I was. Several of them were tired of teaching other kids who were also forced by their parents to take lessons but were less engaged.

Sometimes, tutors were glorified nannies for those kids. So, the tutors loved me and I loved them back. Despite my exhaustion, I felt happy with growing and learning. My days were filled with lessons, and I'd fall into exhausted sleep each night, waking up the next day and repeating the cycle.

But something seemed to be missing. I was friends with pretty much all of my tutors—having no time for friends my age. I hung out with almost no one my age. There was no one to be a child with except my brother.

12

In my childhood, our family went to both Disneyworld and Disneyland once each. This was terrific fun—some of the most fun I've ever had. We queued to take pictures with various Disney characters, rode in the kid strollers that looked like dolphins, and consumed way too much cotton candy. It was a blast!

Our parents also took us to Legoland, Universal Studios, and various other theme parks. I don't have specific memories of these parks as a family anymore, but when I think of theme parks in general, I have a warm glow in my heart. I think of the photos Mom has shown me of our family posing happily together in front of Donald Duck, of us holding hands and analyzing park maps together, plotting our best strategy so as to get the most out of the park.

I've even gone back to some of these theme parks to revisit these parts of my childhood. I still grab a map and strategize the best way to get the most rides, and make sure to eat plenty of the cotton candy.

Arguably one of my favorite things in the world are these parks. They are some of my happy places.

* * *

My family didn't and doesn't really celebrate any Western holidays or special events. When my brother and I were really young, we'd have birthday parties, but past the age of ten mom felt that it was too childish and so this practice ended.

We didn't really do gifts that much. Decorating a tree just felt like work most times. We didn't have an attachment to religion or childhood stories, carols, Santa Claus, or any of it. I think the family can sing Jingle Bells or something if we have the lyrics.

As for Chinese holidays, we really only celebrated Chinese New Year, and we take that one pretty seriously. We'd fly to Shanghai every year and celebrate with Dad's side of the family. We'd feast at fancy restaurants, set off fireworks, watch the national new year show, and all the other traditions.

One year in middle school, I randomly thought of buying flowers for mom. It was Mother's Day. Every day, I biked past the flower shop on my way home and I thought some of them looked nice. I knew Mom liked the big, white lilies.

Dad hadn't ever done anything really for Mother's Day. At school every year they always made us do something, especially in elementary school. I had some cash on me from some previous time Mom and Dad had given me money. So, I counted up the money and jammed it into my pocket, left the house, and biked to the flower shop.

The lady was nice and I liked the bouquets that she'd made, but at school we always made something on our own. I picked out several white lilies and some other random things to stick into a bouquet. I had no idea how to arrange flowers, but the flower lady smiled and bound them up in clear plastic and a neat lavender ribbon for me, so I think I did alright. The bouquet was too big to fit in the basket I had in front of my bike, so I had to hold it awkwardly against my side with an arm over the whole thing. It was then that I thought that perhaps, I'd put too many lilies in it. I kicked off and biked back home with effort, one hand firmly on the handlebars and the other carefully cradling my ridiculous bouquet.

Mom was in the kitchen reading something when I came in. She looked pretty surprised when I opened the front door with the bouquet. I hadn't planned this part, so I didn't really know what to say. Before I could think of anything, Mom howled with laughter. After she calmed down enough to talk, she asked me what I was doing with all those flowers. She teasingly asked if some boy had given those to me, and I bit my cheek hard.

Boys, the most disgusting thing that Mom could have possibly thought of to suggest. Why on earth would I accept flowers from one of *them*? So gross. I grimaced and laid the flowers on the counter in front of her and stomped my way upstairs as I grumbled that they were for her and, "Happy Mother's Day". Mom stopped laughing. I went to my room.

When I came out later, Mom had put them in a vase and even rewrapped the lavender ribbon to be around the vase. She seemed still amused by the whole thing and explained that she wouldn't have guessed that they were for her. The family hadn't celebrated Mother's Day, if it weren't for elementary school teachers' assignments. She hugged me and solemnly thanked me for them. She was happy.

When Dad arrived home, she gushed to him and my brother the story. Before that, I don't remember hearing Dad wishing Mom Happy Mother's Day. I felt good. I felt I'd done a good thing, and my heart swelled up a bit. Each time I passed the living room, I'd look towards the vase for the flowers I'd gotten her. She kept them until they were half dead before she threw them away. I looked forward to the next time I'd pick out the bouquet and buy her flowers.

Every year after that, up until I moved out for college, I bought her bouquets with lots of the big white lilies. Dad and my brother would remember to wish her Happy Mother's Day from the flowers. It kind of became a thing. It felt like family. It felt like happiness.

13

When I had my period, I had these horrible, debilitating cramps. I would sweat, and scream, and writhe around until my body would collapse from exhaustion. Sometimes, the pain was so intense and long-lasting that I would faint. Unlike an instant knockout as I saw in action movies, I would faint very slowly as my body was unable to cope with increasing pain over an extended period of time. Gradually, I would feel my hearing go away and fill with white sound while my vision went dark.

I learned that when my hearing started to go, I did not have long before I fell over unconscious. Luckily, if I was at school, I could perhaps make it to the nurse's office before passing out. I wasn't always successful, but to hide my shame of fainting, I'd at least try to make it to the bathroom and pass out there.

One time, I passed out in the hallway in full view of the senior student lounge. Two seniors helped support each side of me, and together, the three of us awkwardly supported me down the hallway to the nurse's office.

The nurse was always kind; she would give me a hot water bottle and painkillers, and a dark room to cry to myself until the painkillers kicked in and I could sleep to escape from the remaining pain that painkillers couldn't quite take away.

At home, if I was still cramping, I would beg Mom for painkillers. She rarely let me have them. Sometimes she snickered. Sometimes she scolded that it didn't hurt that bad and that I shouldn't be such a baby. She believed it only hurt so much because I was weak, and told me as much. Arguing with her was pointless and would most definitely take away any sliver of hope I might have of getting painkillers, so I said nothing.

Mom would mix up the most awful tasting ginger and hot water concoctions. I felt they didn't help with the pain, but I would down them shakily because she felt that it helped. No position eased me. Holding still hurt about as much as writhing around, but I learned to stay quiet no matter how bad it hurt. I would dig my nails into my palms or into my neck to distract myself from the agony in my lower body, wrap myself tightly in all the covers, and just sweat quietly until I could breathe through the pain and relax a little.

Partially believing mom's criticism of me, I tried to be stronger. At the very least, I learned to put on a braver face, but the pain was still just as unbearable. Sometimes, the pain was so bad I wished that it would just kill me so that I could get it over with. What I didn't realize was that this pain planted an idea in my mind that Mom wasn't always right about everything. After all, how could she know exactly what my body was feeling?

* * *

ONE OF THE CRITICAL METHODS I had of coping with emotional pain in my senior year was Yi. He stroked my hair and dreamily commented that I was beautiful. Sometimes he even added that I was sexy. This was a foreign concept for me. Despite being eighteen and in my senior year of high school, I had not experienced feelings of "beautiful" or "sexy".

Although I did not believe in his remarks, it was nice that he felt that way.

Other female students giggled over guys at school or celebrities they fancied. They'd gawk at magazines and make comments like "Oh, I want to have his babies", or "Oh, he is so cute/sexy/hot". I did not understand the impulse to even think of these things, much less vocalize them. Oftentimes, if we were out and about and they noticed someone who triggered this "he is so cute" reaction in them, they'd suddenly shake each other's shoulders and point out as discreetly as possible at the person of interest. I rarely knew who they were talking about and they'd have to point very obviously in order for me to understand.

They would wear clothes, perfumes, makeup, creams and powders—things I didn't understand and hadn't any interest in. They would flip through pictures of actresses or singers they found to be "beautiful" or "sexy" and try to sing their songs, wear their clothes, and adopt their sayings. It all seemed like a lot of work to me. I felt overwhelmed by the whole concept and opted to only dress up for prom and other special occasions. I rejected dresses, makeup, perfume, and the rest because I didn't understand their purpose. I typically just dragged out of my dresser whatever was at the top of the pile.

Other than being clueless about clothes, I also didn't know what to do with my hair beyond scooping it into a ponytail. In middle school, I wore a ponytail with a large scrunchy wrapped around it so much so that my friends nicknamed me "eighth note". This was because the eighth note had a flag on the note notation, and my swishing high ponytail and my being in the choir made the nickname stick. On days where I was being silly or empty headed, they'd call me whole note as a joke.

Other students in my grade had outgrown things like tag and playing at the playground and were moving on to having crushes on one another. But I still found boys to be like potatoes; they existed, but they had just about the same level of appeal to me. I bonded better with students a couple years younger than me and at lunch or recess times, we would eat together and then they'd steal my scrunchy.

That was our game. They would steal my scrunchy and begin a game of "monkey in the middle" where the "monkey" in the middle attempted to recover the item being passed around by the others. I was always the "monkey". They would giggle uproariously as we raced through the cafeteria to burst outside onto the playground. I'd chase them until we were all tired of playing and they would return my scrunchy to me if I had been unsuccessful, which was true most of the time. I would mock-indignantly reattach it to my ponytail, and we'd all be giggling again. Then we'd breathlessly rush off to our next classes.

I looked forward to meeting them as they greeted me at my locker every morning. Together, they'd accompany me to my classes. When I went into ninth grade and no longer shared the same lunchtime as them, they still kept waiting by my locker each morning, even though our different lunch times meant that we couldn't play "monkey in the middle" anymore.

14

I did not understand physical or sexual attraction, perhaps because I was a late bloomer. It was completely foreign and alien to me. I personally did not experience feelings of physical or sexual attraction at all.

One time, there was a talent show and a small group of us decided to do some choreographed Latin dancing as a performance. There were three couples in total, including myself and my dance partner. We wore our Latin dancing dresses, put on Latin dancing shoes, took classes together, and practiced together for a few months. The audition went smoothly and the actual performance was the same.

As we walked off the stage, one of the stage crew students motioned me to help pick up a dark cloth that had not been cleared from a previous act in the talent show. She was hidden in the wings, and I was still in full view of the audience, as was the cloth. It didn't occur to me to even think about it; someone was asking me to help pick something up and it was on my way, so I swiftly bent down and picked it up. This drew immediate whistles and giggling from the audience. Startled, I strode the rest of the few steps out of audience view and behind the curtains a bit faster than my original pace.

I checked to see if I had perhaps ripped my dress and that was what people were whistling and giggling at. But my dress was not ripped; there was nothing wrong with it, and everything was in place. I even bent over the same way again in the changing room to check in the mirror. But I didn't see anything out of the ordinary.

Puzzled, I asked anxiously what the audience had giggled about. My dance mates explained that it was a very sexy Latin dress and that in bending over I had no choice but to stick out my bum. The boys had been whistling and chuckling about it.

My bum? Why did that matter? Everyone had a bum. I didn't get it. Was my bum a weird shape? I didn't think so. And as for the dress. Sexy? I thought of it as a uniform, similar to how policemen, judges, or various professionals typically wear uniforms. This was simply the uniform for Latin dancing. It was merely the correct dress to go with the matching activity.

15

My blindness was not only just about my own body, but also for people around me. I had no awareness or appreciation of physical appeal. I noticed if someone wore matching clothes or a cool outfit, but I could not understand when my peers described people's bodies or faces has hot, cute, or sexy. My classmates could not believe that I had no radar for any of that, desperately rattling off lists of supposedly high physical appeal actors, actresses, and models but to no avail. I had no reaction. It was as if I was missing a key sense, such as touch or smell.

Eventually, I began to develop an understanding of attraction through studying. I read about how people value symmetry in someone's face and body. I learned about how we are biologically wired to be attracted to certain physical traits and how cultural and historical influences affect our judgment on the matter. And through personal experience of hugging people, I've developed an appreciation of a certain amount of muscle and fat in a person. That isn't so much due to visual appearance as much as my preference in firmness, such as in choosing the right pillow.

It didn't seem disadvantageous to not have a reaction to anyone's visual appeal except that sometimes I stood out if I asked questions for someone to explain why they felt attracted to someone else. They would find it odd that I didn't have the same reaction, and my earnest questions in an attempt to understand, seemed alien. I learned to stop asking questions and used my evidence-based way to understand attraction. To fit in, I sometimes mimicked the reactions of others if I noticed several people having the same reaction.

Evidence-based visual appeal meant I eventually developed a socially acceptable eye for beauty. If I saw that someone's features were symmetrical and they had a youthful complexion, I would guess that they were considered conventionally attractive. I knew that certain makeup styles were considered to be pretty, and so I could identify those as well. When I started studying art, I learned some ratios of facial features that made someone attractive—size of nose or lips in relation to general size of face, size of head to the rest of the body, and so on and so forth. I recorded various physical details of people I saw in a very unemotional, factual way.

I felt drawn to no one merely on a physical level. I would instead draw guesses or conclusions about how much they cared about their health, diet, and fitness, ranging from recklessness or uncaring to caring perhaps too much for my lifestyle when choosing partners.

16

Unsurprisingly, this created challenges in my relationship with Yi. On a spontaneous date, he had taken a long taxi ride to come closer to where I lived and met me in secret at an ice cream shop. We ordered a scoop each and walked to the cashier lady and he paid for our orders. When we sat down at a round table to eat our ice cream, Yi abruptly put his head down on the table. I was confused and poked his arm to ask if he was alright.

Mumbling into the table, he said he had known this would be an issue, that he couldn't watch me eat ice cream. This didn't make any sense to me. We had eaten food together before, why was this any different? And why would eating anything cause this kind of response? So, I happily licked away at my ice cream without much thought beyond the sweet and cold qualities of the ice cream.

When I found out a couple months later by force what act it reminded him of—what he imagined me licking—I finally understood. I did not eat ice cream again for a very long time. And when I did, I ate ice cream alone so that no one would see me and think of that.

17

One time, when I was about twelve years old, a colleague of Dad's at some dinner or something bent down to my height and observed aloud that I was beautiful. I was so happy. I was beautiful!

Wanting to share that glorious feeling, I excitedly pulled at Dad's sleeve. Knowing he would be irritated if I spoke to him within earshot of other adults, I asked him if I could have a private word with him. Looking around and noticing no one too close by, he leaned over slightly to give his attention. I had barely finished describing what had happened when he snorted, "Of course he told you you're beautiful, he wants your Dad's money".

The word "beautiful" turned to acid. Even today, so many years later, I question compliments that I am given. I sometimes literally interview the person who gave me the compliment to discover the motive for praise or evidence to support their statement. It is challenging for me to accept these compliments. The most I can do is try to mask my mixed feelings with a polite smile and thank you.

18

What is "beautiful", anyways? What does it mean to be beautiful? Beauty was a constantly shifting thing that I couldn't fathom. In my childhood, some days I would be beautiful, Mom and Dad would exclaim how beautiful I was. They would comment on my hair, my skin, my body. Sometimes, Mom would even sigh and ramble on that she was jealous of various features that I had, such as the thickness of my hair, or that I had such youthful and pale skin.

Other days, through hissing and spitting, she drilled into me that I was ugly—the ugliest beast, a demon, a monster, no one could ever possibly want me as a friend, a lover, a wife. I was the worst. This changed so frequently and without logic or warning that I largely gave up on developing a personal view of what beauty meant or was.

As a kid, I stopped believing in my own perceptions of beauty or thinking about it because Mom and Dad were making that judgement and my opinion really did not matter. It's possible that this parenting was a significant factor in me developing my evidence-based attraction.

When I was growing up under their roof, all I knew was that I had no idea what beauty meant except that it was tied to whatever Mom and Dad said it was at that moment. To be consistently beautiful in their eyes and by their definition, seemed impossible. And so, I made no attempts to diet or lower my weight, accepting my "fatness" and "ugliness" or "beauty". In addition, since I had not yet experienced any desire to attract anyone—male or female—as so many other girls my age had begun to try, it really didn't bother me if I was fat or ugly or pretty. I did not understand any functional benefit of being attractive or not, and I didn't think I had much control over it; so, what was the point?

Traditional Chinese values for female beauty included having pale skin (being tan or darker skinned was associated with poor or uneducated people), being extremely thin and weak (this made men feel bigger and manlier and have more lifting and carrying to do since the women were twigs), and being meek or submissive (theoretically, this would allow men to feel more masculine). In other words, this was how to be beautiful in both body and mind.

I knew that I was pale, so there was that. My grandma would worry about me getting dark from going outside. If I was heading out, she'd stop me at the door and try to hand me a parasol so that I would use it to protect my skin from the sun. When I was younger, I'd refuse and we'd quarrel. As I grew older and didn't want to distress her, I'd take it with me and carry it around all day under my arm, but I couldn't actually be bothered to use it. Luckily, I never picked up enough color for her to call me out on it.

A few times, dad bought me whitening cream. After purchasing the gift though, he felt that he had stepped into female territory too much. He was too uncomfortable to talk about skincare or using the cream. Instead, he just handed it to me and implied that I ought to use it. Mom didn't think that the stuff worked, preferring instead to monitor my outside activities.

I was fat by Chinese standards. Too tall. Too muscly. I was fat because I was 120-130lb 5'6 when the average height for women was 5'1 and for men it was 5'6. I was as tall as the average man, which meant most men had to look me in the eye. The ideal height and weight for an attractive woman was to be 5'2 and 100lb. I did not consider it to be possible for me to be 100lb, so I surrendered to being "fat".

Mom would occasionally stress out about how I was going to find a man who would want me. She felt it very important that the man must be taller and impressed this on me as a young adult. She would fret about me growing taller than 5'6 and prayed that I didn't gain any more weight. Sometimes, she'd wistfully sigh and wished my brother and I would swap heights since I was taller than him. She was worried he'd never achieve an ideal male height, and therefore have difficulty finding a girlfriend or wife. He was shorter and scrawnier than I was for the longest time.

I wasn't actually muscular in my eyes, but to Mom and Dad I was dangerously muscular. To deter me from working out, exercising, or engaging in activities that might develop my muscles, they would emphasize that if my muscles grew too big "no one would want me". I would be very unattractive. I thought it was ridiculous and never heeded it, but that didn't stop them from threatening me as if it would.

What I did know was that being "fat" and "too tall" and "ugly" presented some difficulties growing up in China. After I hit my last growth spurt, buying clothing and shoes was very difficult. Many department stores—Chinese equivalent of a Macy's or something—did not carry my size of shoes or pants. I would either have to shop in the men's section for shoes which Mom found horribly embarrassing, or custom order certain sizes.

I was largely uninterested in shopping, preferring to read or play games on my Gameboy while Mom picked items out for me. I trusted her sense of fashion more than my own from years of her complaining that my stylistic choices were poor. So, when we went shopping, I was basically a mobile mannequin that shuffled alongside her. I sat where she told me to sit, tried on whatever she told me to try on.

Shopping was a chore. For tops, Mom could zip around and pick items out that she thought I should wear, but for pants and shoes, we learned to go straight to a shopkeeper and ask if they carried my sizes. A surprised shopkeeper would either stammer that they didn't carry those sizes, or that there were only very few choices available. It was far more efficient to look at the few items that the shopkeeper would bring before us and then move on to the next shop.

Considering labor in China was and still is pretty cheap, we opted to custom order often, so mom would have me measured and order shoes and pants that would fit me. When I came to America, I learned that the size equivalent I was for shoes was a size 9 (one of the most common shoe sizes in America for women, the other one being size 6). For pants I was a size 5-6 or basically, a small/medium depending on the brand. However, in China, I was a circus freak and needed to custom order clothing for anything to fit.

One of the recurring issues Mom and Dad had with me was my "attitude". When I was a child, I was typically obedient. I ate what was put in front of me, didn't really fight bedtimes, wore what they gave me, and did as I was instructed. However, approaching eighteen and after that, I began to question more and more their parenting decisions. This was in large part due to the fact that I was influenced by exposure to the international community and American/Western culture.

There was a great deal of culture clash at home. Mom and Dad were very influenced by old Confucian theories, and unfortunately, especially neo-Confucianism has some pretty sexist sayings about women. I'll share translated ones here:

"When young, a woman should obey the father, when married, the husband, when old, the son."

"A woman's duty is not to control or take charge."

"Woman's greatest duty is to produce a son."

"A woman ruler is like a hen crowing."

"Disorder is not sent down by Heaven, it is produced by women."

"There are three unfilial acts: the greatest of these is the failure to produce sons."

"Women are to be led and to follow others."

"Women's nature is passive."

"A woman should look on her husband as if he were Heaven itself, and ever thinking how she may yield to him."

Despite how strongly they were influenced by Confucianism, I was more strongly influenced by the international community from the international school I had been going to. Later on, I was also transformed by being in college in America. Much to their dismay, our differing views would bring more and more friction to our relationship as I grew older.

Through increasingly toxic arguments, Mom and Dad presumed that my aggressive attitude towards them must be the way I was to everyone. So, they further irritated me by often forwarding me emails about how to be a better and more likeable person, which only pushed me away more and worsened my feelings towards them. It was a vicious cycle that spiraled out of control over the years. They wondered several times aloud how I managed to get any boyfriends or just friends. They even communicated this with my brother and he asked me innocently and seriously once about one of my more serious boyfriends, "What does he see in you?"

19

And yet, as undesirable as I was, here I was with Yi, my boyfriend. And he felt I was beautiful. He remarked I was so beautiful and sexy that it made him want to have sex with me, whether I wanted to or not. Not knowing any better, I thought this was romantic.

I was a pinball. Mom and Dad would spew poison on me, repeating until I was half hypnotized and brainwashed with how undesirable and horrible I was. I'd hold my tears and pour my heart out on Yi's shoulder, and then he'd brainwash me about what sex was and proceed in raping me. I stopped resisting him after a while, because I believed maybe all sex was like this. I didn't know any better, and despite the physical pain, it felt less painful than listening to Mom and Dad. And if I couldn't stand either side, I'd just zone everything out by studying and working on schoolwork.

Several months of this later though, I couldn't cope anymore. I could feel myself falling apart. I was torn. I didn't want to please Mom and Dad because I hated them. I wanted to perform well in school, but performing well in school pleased Mom and Dad. I wanted to be a good girlfriend to Yi, so he would keep loving me, but I struggled to force myself to enjoy what he called sex. I couldn't reconcile these things in my world. It was ripping me apart. I had to find another way.

And I did. I came up with this idea of delayed suicide. I would perform well in school, because I wanted to and because it pleased Mom and Dad. I would live by their standards and make them believe I was this golden child; I would make them happy, I would make their dreams come true, try my best to do all the things they trained me to do, and definitely put an end to the dating Yi part after starting college. And then, when I had accomplished it all, working a job with a level of pay that impressed them, I would take it all away. I would take myself out of this world at the peak of my existence. I wanted to fill them with joy so that I could create the maximum amount of pain for them. Yi became less and less important as I clung to this satisfying dream of their pain and horror for when I left this world. I eagerly tackled my schoolwork as a part of my plan.

Although I didn't write down a specific year I was going to die or an exact way I would achieve that, I didn't worry about the details. Just knowing that I could hurt them, created a warm glow in my heart, a tiny flame that carried me through all hardships. Thinking about suicide, I didn't feel sad or as though I was missing out or hurting others beyond Mom and Dad. I could not fathom why anyone else would care about my insignificant existence. And even if they did, the function that I served as a friend was dispensable and easily replaceable as I had been told time and again by Mom and Dad. I just wanted to hurt Mom and Dad as much as I possibly could.

20

One of the questions survivors get asked is why stay after the first violent encounter? Wouldn't the first time make me want to stop being with Yi? I just felt so mixed up and lost. When Yi observed aloud that I was "being weird" for not liking sex and that he was actually quite good at it, I felt that I should believe him. After all, I was inexperienced and in my first relationship, and my first sexual experience, where he had much more relationship, life, and sexual experience than me. I did not know and therefore did not process that this first time was criminal.

I didn't trust my own judgement. I would have turned to Mom and Dad or at least Mom for some perspective or advice, but the way they had reacted to the news that I was dating Yi had made that impossible. I felt that I could not go near Mom and Dad without pissing them off. They felt I was bringing them shame by dating Yi and told me my presence constantly reminded them of all the time and money they had wasted in raising me. I avoided them and hid in my room whenever I was home.

Yi expressed that I was strange for crying during and after my first time. It was supposed to be an enjoyable experience, he stated, "people love to have sex". He seemed genuinely perplexed and commented that I was the only person he'd ever slept with that had reacted in this way.

Considering I had only done it once and with one person, who was I to say what sex was supposed to be like?

What if it was because I was not doing things right? What if it was my fault? What if I was bad at sex and that's why the first experience had been so awful? I couldn't trust my opinions and feelings. I didn't want to be an outlier, I didn't want to be weird. He advised that if I enjoyed it more or behaved a certain way during sex with him, then it would hurt less. He apologized for being a "little rough" but explained that he lost control because of how much he desired me. I guess he felt that this explanation made it ok, since he was still expressing how much he wanted me.

Rape is the "penetration, no matter how slight, of the vagina or anus with any body part or object, or oral penetration by a sex organ of another person, without the consent of the victim."—United States Department of Justice

But I didn't know the word "rape". It quite literally didn't exist in my dictionary at that time. I had not been taught much about sex, let alone that there was this word "rape". It did not occur to me that someone would force anyone in this way. I thought that what had just happened, was normal sex, since parts of it fit with how others had described to me. People said it "hurt the first time" people said it was "kind of scary", people said that "you always bleed the first time".

When Yi was finally done with me that first night, we got in a cab; he dropped me off at the subway station and I went home. I had Latin dancing class that afternoon in preparation for the Talent Show. I felt sore and detached, but I focused as much as I could on the class, following the steps, following my partner's lead, doing the best that I could. Not knowing what to do after class, but knowing that there were always homework assignments to work on and tests to study for, I went up to my room and pulled out my textbooks to do more schoolwork.

From then on, almost every time we went on dates, we would wind up at his place or at a hotel and he would have sex with my body. He stated that it frustrated him when I didn't enjoy the experience. He said that sometimes, that was what made him hurt me.

I learned to distance myself mentally, make the sounds that he liked, tense my muscles, and behave the way he wanted me to. And he was right, I hurt less when I behaved the "right" way—the way he wanted. And I didn't want to be hurt anymore, because it could hurt a lot. So, I became really good at doing what he trained me to do.

I couldn't stop myself crying or fighting the first several times, but after a while, I learned how to be a better sexual partner.

Everyone has a breaking point; I lost count how many times it took for me to reach my own. How many times did my body fight back instinctually even though my mind didn't know how to or why, since I was destined to lose; ten times? Twenty times? Forty times? It didn't matter. Eventually, the lesson was burned into my brain. I knew I would never defeat him; my only option was to submit. Submitting was easier than fighting. And more importantly, submitting meant less pain. Submitting meant that Yi would be happy with me and would comfort me about school and home life.

So, I tried to like what Yi did to me. It sounds really messed up, because I was trying to find physical and emotional pleasure from him raping me. He instructed me it should be physically and emotionally pleasurable, and that "everyone else" found physical and emotional pleasure in sex. I didn't want to be an outcast. I didn't want to be behaving in the "wrong" way.

I didn't want to be the only one not doing sex right. I was a teenager trying to fit in. I was trying to be a good girlfriend so he wouldn't abandon me. I thought that, maybe if I was good enough, he wouldn't turn on me like Mom and Dad did. I didn't want him to be displeased or disappointed with me.

He coached me in how to be a better partner for him, and I learned like a robot, since I had no sexual drive or interest in any of the physically intimate acts he seemed so interested in. But just like with my tutoring lessons, I always tried hard to please. At first, his lessons weren't too hard. He wanted me to place my body a certain way, arch my back, kiss him a certain way, stroke his back, his shoulders, his legs. He wanted me to dress a certain way, wear my hair a certain way. And I complied.

He insisted that I should not talk to anyone about us—about what we were doing. He stated that he had all the answers and I believed him. He was older than me, worldlier, more experienced.

One time, I made the mistake of talking to another man, just platonically. It was a work colleague of Yi's who sold snowboards, and I was just asking him some questions about snowboarding out of curiosity. Yi beat up his work colleague. I saw the bruises and was horrified. From then on, his work colleagues and friends learned to not talk to me unless he was around, and even then, to be careful.

I cried. I hadn't meant for anyone to be hurt from what I had thought was a harmless conversation. I felt horribly guilty. It didn't occur to me that this wasn't normal or that it wasn't my fault. All I knew is that someone had gotten hurt in connection with my actions. I withdrew from all of his friends and even my school friends.

* * *

AS LONG AS YI WAS HAPPY WITH ME, he would take me out on dates, we would do fun things, silly things, things I enjoyed. If I was a good girl, we'd go out on the lake in a paddle boat and I could blow bubbles over the water. I loved doing that. Yi would take me to my favorite restaurants, whisper nice things to me.

Then one day, he asked me to kiss it, his penis. And I hadn't done that before. And I couldn't. All my training fell away and I started shaking uncontrollably.

I could not. I could not do this.

He gripped my hair painfully and pushed me down his body with a smoothness that reminded me of his awful muscular strength and how much weaker I was. He held my hair so that my face was right over him. But I still couldn't, and my neck muscles were locked tight as I vibrated with horror.

Despite Mom's hatred of crying, the self-control I had developed over the years, and Yi's conditioning of me up to that point, I began to weep. I'd learned to tear quietly, so I don't know if he saw or heard my tears. I didn't dare look up at his face even if I had been capable of doing so.

I had the sheets balled into my fists as I silently resisted his command—if only for a moment. Sweating with effort, I knew that his way would be the inevitable way. Sure enough, after being amused by my futile struggles, he grew impatient and started pulling me closer to him. And there was a tiny cry, so small that I think I might have imagined it as it left me, and that was the last time I resisted him. There was no other option. This was the price I had to pay for his comfort. I had already chosen between the abuse of Mom and Dad and the abuse that he doled out and he knew this. He knew I needed the emotional support he offered me outside of sex. He could have asked me to do anything, and regardless of how many tears, he would have eventually had his way. And he knew all of that.

So, I learned what he asked of me. I licked, I kissed, I stroked, and I pushed myself deep into a dark well in my mind until I could barely feel or see anything happening around me. Over the months, like a programmer and my body the machine, I coded in the moans, the words, the muscle spasms, all of it, until it took no effort, no thought, to do what he wanted. And it seemed to make him happy, so it worked.

Eventually, all it took was one lust-filled look in his eyes and I would be his perfect sex toy. I obeyed. I learned to black out my mind and run the "sex program" until he was satisfied.

It might not make sense to anyone else, but at the time, I felt that it was a trade—fair or not fair, it didn't matter. It was necessary.

Mom and Dad's near constant verbal and emotional abuse was destroying me. They expounded frequently on how I was worthless and I almost believed them if it weren't for Yi. As long as Yi found use for my body, as long as I was "rape-worthy", I was still worth something, if only for this. I was still worthy of breathing air and drinking water. So, in a way, the rape and sexual abuse I experienced gave me a sense of worth that I wouldn't have had otherwise.

Before I came up with my suicide plan, I couldn't let go of him. I couldn't leave. Just like how Mom and Dad had raised me with justifications for their abusive behaviors, Yi both hurt me and healed me. Yi held me in his arms when I cried and held me down other times.

And through all this, September and the promise of a better life in college creeped closer.

21

A year before I met Yi, an innocent question inspired by biology class led me to learn a lot about the months leading up to when I was born.

I was in my junior year in high school in IB Higher Level Biology class and the subject at the time was the reproductive system. As a result, we learned about how babies were made, the various organs involved, and we even did some dissections on rabbit and cow reproductive organs. As part of the class, since there was no sex ed requirement at the school, I suppose our teacher felt that it was her responsibility to educate us a little bit about it. Therefore, there was one lecture on various methods of contraception.

One of the things she mentioned was "family planning", "the practice of controlling the number of children in a family and the intervals between their births". In other words, planning when to have kids, how many, and when.

Being a curious child, I decided I would ask Mom and Dad if they had used family planning in having myself and my brother. Mom, after I explained what the term meant, very matter-of-factly said that there was no planning in having me and that I had been an accident, a mistake. She admitted that she didn't even want me at first, but Dad was soon to be passing the Chinese socially acceptable age to have kids, and so she grudgingly kept me. She babbled all of this seemingly as a stream of consciousness, just rolling off her tongue without much thought as she reminisced about the past.

Before I could even process this information, she rambled on, talking about how she had resented me when I was first growing inside of her. I had made her feel sick and miss home. I reminded her of how, if she had still been in China, in Chinese culture she would have been surrounded by friends and family. There would have been lots of people helping to take care of her and pampering her. Instead she was in the US and taking care of herself as best she could. Dad didn't help much—both out of ignorance, a lack of empathy, and being too busy with his PhD studies.

Mom was in the middle of her US undergraduate degree (her Chinese undergraduate degree was not recognized in US at the time), and realized with dread that I would soon disrupt things. Originally, she, in her words "naively", thought that she would be able to return to school after I was born. However, between the costs of my existence, tuition, and other living expenses, it was decided that mom could not continue her degree.

She wept bitterly. In response to my birth, Dad threw himself at work and school in a frenzy, helping very little with direct baby care. He felt it was best to quickly find a job that paid more so that he could make sure to bring back enough dough to feed the family. He did not want me to grow up as starved and disadvantaged as he had been as a child. Furthermore, in his mind, it was a woman's job to raise children; anything that he did in terms of direct baby care was like a gift to mom.

Stubbornly, Mom still wanted to complete her course credits at least for that semester. As her body grew with me inside her, she declared her resolve to skeptical professors that she would complete that semester's courses that had already been paid for. She went to class until she was too large and close to my birth week to do so.

The first month was incredibly hard with a lot to adjust to, as it is for any new parents. But after the first month of my arrival, she felt she had some of the baby care under her belt. She felt more confident about feeding the baby on time, burping the baby, and various other daily baby tasks. Wearily, she flipped open a textbook for the first time since my delivery to see if she could do some reading.

I had been born in March, so the semester was still going. She needed to catch up for missed classes and schoolwork. Even without a baby in her care, this would have been a challenging task.

And it was not to be. Mom's spirit died a little when I started wailing for attention. She had barely finished a page. Doggedly, she went back and forth between me and the textbook, eventually breaking down in rage and hopelessness. She said she never opened her textbooks again after that. Taking one last look at the cover, she put it away and resigned herself to being my caregiver, resigned herself to being a mother and a wife, to forever support Dad and his career, till death do us part.

22

Unsurprisingly, since Mom considered herself to be robbed of her American college experience as well as adult life in general, she took it very seriously when it came time for me to apply to various colleges. She poured through articles and lists of rankings of schools, read about various majors, and frantically tried to plot my future.

I looked at classes I had done well in, but was not able to decide on anything. Just because I had received an A grade in a particular class, did that mean I wanted to spend the rest of my life doing that?

I would lie in bed and think of what life would be like if I pursued this major or that. What would waking up each day be like? What would work be like? What would life be like as an adult? I didn't have a clue. I only knew how Mom described her life. And she described her life as hell.

Mom ranted to me often that her life was entirely revolved around Dad, myself, and my brother. She would sometimes confide in me that she "didn't have a life" or that this "didn't count as a life" or "what kind of life is this". I never had the answer. She complained to me about Dad's parents treating her coldly when I was born, because I was a girl and not a boy. Although things improved when my brother was born, she ranted to me about them being frosty when there were disagreements on how to raise us kids.

When my brother or I had a bad grade, she would yell and rage that our grade was her grade as a mother and that everyone would judge her or treat her differently if we didn't perform up to standard, which was all A's. She relayed to me that all the relatives talked; all the other parents talked, and that there was constant competition. If I didn't want her to feel ashamed or depressed, I had to do well in school.

The pressure was insane. She sounded like a hostage with the rest of the community and family, having a gun at her head to make sure we performed. Most of the time, I was under pressure to "save" her, since my brother's grades and school performance were not so good. I cared less about this when I entered college, but most of the years growing up I felt compelled to "save" her.

* * *

DAD'S LIFE WAS MOSTLY A MYSTERY. I knew that, as a businessman, he often enjoyed dining and drinking richly. His life outside of the home was full of expensive restaurants and hotels, trips around the world, flying first class or on the company jet and even helicopter occasionally. The longest time he was ever gone was a whole six months.

According to mom, even when he was home, he was pretty uninvolved so sometimes I didn't really notice. When I was young, Dad's initial thinking about parenting was that it was the woman's job. His job was to bring back money and pay the bills and provide. So, he'd come home from work, change from work outfit into sweats, and watch TV.

He watched TV enough that I never developed a TV watching habit since he always took over the TV remote controller on evenings when he was home. He liked to watch the news or golf or tennis—none of which were interesting to me when I was a kid and to this day.

Sometimes, Dad made an effort to educate me about what his work life was like. He'd bring me to the shiny business tower that he worked in. We'd ride the elevator to the floor he worked on and he'd bring me by the windows with the best views, which of course included his windowed, private office. He'd introduce me to the maid staffed on that floor, instructing her to provide me with fruits or water or snacks if I requested. Then he'd usher me to an empty, unused office where he'd drop me off to amuse myself or study or something, ambling over to his office after saying hello to everyone.

Sometimes, he'd let me hang out in his office so that I could type for him while he dictated. It was one of the things that he loved doing. He felt that since my brother and I were raised learning English from a younger age than he had, that we definitely had a better grasp of the language than he did. He'd dictate word for word the whole email, asking me to type it up with my "quick fingers" since I was faster than him.

It wasn't until his mid-50s that we finally got him to type with home-row keys instead of punching in letters with his pointer fingers. He'd agonize or go over each sentence, running his choice of this adjective or that noun over and over to make sure the email was exactly the way he wanted. Oftentimes, it took us close to half an hour to finally reach the point of him being comfortable hitting the send button for a four-sentence email. This work life seemed rather unappealing.

Despite being uninterested in his work life, I always admired Dad's ability as a businessman. The impression I got was that he was always a superhero in the company, irreplaceable where others came and went, receiving promotions even when the company was laying off others, having the nice office and furniture, receiving the company car he wanted, as well as all sorts of other nice company perks. All his colleagues had something nice to say about him—not that they would have ever said anything negative to me.

Over the years, Dad had become a formidable businessman, greatly respected and amazingly connected. Whenever I had a question about any industry or country, he knew people there; successful and accomplished people who were also well connected. He boasted about shaking hands with world leaders and CEOs. His name was on many billion-dollar deals. He even appeared in some news articles here and there.

Dad was a rock star at work, but home life was a different story. When we were kids, Dad didn't really know what to get us or what to do with us.

I distinctly recall one time in my teenage years I was just babbling away about how my new favorite drink was almond milk. Keeping in mind that Dad's work was in petroleum, upstream oil and gas drilling and discovery, Dad somehow made a deal with a large almond milk producing company. So, he came home from a business trip with multiple crates of almond milk and said that since my favorite drink was almond milk, he had made a great deal with an almond milk company and had, in his words, secured a lifetime supply of almond milk. Of course, I then went and excitedly drank so much of the stuff that I puked in the bathroom and was so horribly disgusted by the taste of the milk after the puking incident, that I couldn't be near the stuff for a couple years without gagging.

23

After work, most days Dad would get a massage before returning home. Mom privately complained about this habit of his to me. She felt it kept him from coming home sooner. She confided in me occasionally about their marital issues, starting around the age of eleven. I was exasperatedly trying to do my homework while she paced around and hissed about his massages, ranting to me about her frustrations. She could not understand why he had to go so often and why he didn't want to talk about why he went so often. Over time, Mom began to suspect that perhaps "massage" was actually something else but she wasn't sure.

Randomly, I remarked "Why not check his work bag?" Mom was so trusting, she never checked his bag. But I guess my idea got under her skin.

Dad was not very sneaky. She found cards that belonged to prostitutes in the main pouch of his bag. She burst into my room with the cards in hand and flung them in rage. The brightly colored business cards of prostitutes fluttered to the floor. I'd never seen one before.

Mom was freaking out. Not only did she feel heartbroken and betrayed, but she also feared that she might have STDs. I didn't know what STDs even meant. She described STDs in very vague terms, but from what she revealed to me, I felt a huge amount of disgust. I did not want to touch Dad in case it was catching.

For a while, the pattern became such that I would go to school, come back, do homework in my room, and she'd stomp in, slam the door, and rant and rave about how upset she was with Dad. School was out about 3:30, and I'd arrive home—depending on after school activities—around 4-5pm. Dad wouldn't be home until about 6pm if he didn't have a dinner scheduled, and if he did have a dinner or a "massage" scheduled, then we wouldn't see him until later. After that, he'd be stationed on the couch watching TV.

This gave Mom ample time to work through her feelings with me while I worked through math problems. She vented to me about wanting to divorce him and how she'd confided in her Mom and how Grandma was extremely upset and that Grandma couldn't be upset because Grandma had health problems and the stress would lower her immune system even more. Mom wept that she couldn't handle it all.

While she figured out how she would confront him, she continued searching through Dad's things. She checked his phone another night, and saw numbers saved with prostitute-like names, screaming the names at me one by one. The names all seemed forgettably generic to me—names like "Kitty" or "Bunny", but they were branded into her mind.

She broke down repeatedly in my room after school while my pencil continued moving through math problems. Listening to the sound of the pencil scratches and her sobbed out words, I understood the concept of "cheating" for the first time.

Sometimes, she asked me who I would choose to stay with if they divorced. This was a big question for me. I knew that Dad made the money, but Dad wasn't much for parenting. Eventually, I figured if they truly did separate, my younger brother absolutely had to stay with mom. I said to continue my education and make sure I could financially have the option of going to good schools and such, I should probably stay with Dad. And in this way, neither of them would be lonely, I explained.

I was never sure of what I should do or say to comfort Mom in this time. I felt terrible and guilty that I had been the one who had started this avalanche of emotions by suggesting that she check Dad's work bag.

Sometimes, my brother and I would hear them shouting at each other. One time, the shouting was so bad that my brother and I came downstairs hand-in-hand and we begged them to stop. Dad never liked us kids seeing them fight, so he would make a point to forcefully pull Mom into a hug as if to say "See? Everything's fine," even though everything wasn't fine.

Eventually, things calmed down. Mom told me it was a combination of factors that led to her deciding to let things go after dad promised not to get a mistress. She explained that she worried about us kids and how we would handle a divorce or separation. She talked about money and worried she would not be able to provide enough to care for us.

She also shared that she had reached out to other housewives that were her friends. They had told her that it was actually quite prevalent among the husbands to seek prostitutes for their sexual needs.

Once confronted, Dad snitched and told Mom a whole list of husbands who were guilty of seeing prostitutes also. In a way, it was so common, that it was "normal". Mom said under the weight of all this, she decided to let it all go and continue life as if it never happened. She made me promise not to tell my brother; she said he was too young to handle this information and that it would crush him.

I obediently never talked to my brother about it.

24

My brother and I were very close when we were little. Mom fondly recalls an image of me when I was a toddler. I'd press my face against the screen door looking out onto the street. I looked at the other children playing with their siblings and I sighed mightily and asked Mom if I could get a big brother. She chortled that it didn't work that way, but unbeknownst to me, she and Dad had planned to have another child all along.

To produce a boy in the family was something that Chinese people had always coveted. Pressure became much more intense with the advent of the famous single-child-policy in 1979. This government plan called for "families to have one child each in order to curb a then-surging population and its corresponding consumption of resources". One of the unfortunate side effects of this plan was that families panicked over the possibility that they might not produce a male as their single child. This was such a huge concern that although it was illegal to have sex-selective abortions, the reality is that somehow the sex ratio of male to female became more and more skewed.

Being born in the US meant that technically, as long as any babies born of Mom and Dad did not claim Chinese citizenship, this rule would not apply. In other words, my parents could have as many children as they wanted since this policy only applied to Chinese babies. However, cultural pressures from China extended all the way across the ocean to their tiny apartment in the US. As mentioned before, the first time Dad could afford to bring his parents over for an extended visit after I was born, Mom claimed they treated her less well because I was a female and not a male child.

Luckily, once Dad was earning a decent income and had finished getting his PhD, they decided they could easily afford a second child and should do so in the hopes that it would be a boy. And so, my brother was born. Mom's status and quality of life improved a good deal, Dad was overjoyed and so was I. I now had a brother!

I was so excited to have this baby brother that, for a "show-and-tell" in kindergarten, I begged and pleaded with Mom so that I could bring him. "Show-and-tell" was typically a task at school for children to bring and present an item to the class. My brother was the most adorable and precious thing in the world to me, and I could think of nothing better to bring.

The teacher and Mom thought my passion was very cute, and so Mom, instead of dropping me off at school and leaving, hauled my brother into the class in his car seat for me to display to my classmates as I waxed on about how amazing it was to have this baby brother. Mom chuckles about the memory of how protective and possessive I was of him. Hovering my arms over him, I emphasized to my class that this was a show-and-tell only, and that no one could touch him.

As my brother grew to be more than just a baby stuck in a car seat and developed some motor functionality, we played together more and more. I happily shared with him my puzzles and my dolls.

Mom and Dad feared any influence that might cause my brother to be gay or less masculine, so our attention was turned towards more "masculine" toys. Dad was making much better money than the barely-scraping-by money he had been making when I was born, and could therefore afford better toys. He began to get us car related toys and even Lego sets, believing these to be better for my brother. The dolls quietly disappeared.

With the Lego sets, my brother liked to have the step-by-step instructions in between the two of us as we sat on the floor. I would sort through the pieces and like an assembly line, he'd call for the next pieces that he needed and I would find them or line them up in the order he would need them. He would click the pieces together and we would efficiently construct each Lego set.

We were very close in these early years. After I hit my first major growth spurt and he was quite a deal smaller than I was, I'd often give him piggy back rides around since he was only half my size. In many of our family photos, he is on my back in this way.

Yet, in this closeness there was some sibling fighting as well. Part of the fighting was normal sibling squabbles, but part was also influenced by Mom and Dad. Mom and Dad wanted us to be competitive and pursue excellence, always pushing us to be better. One of the ways that they did this was to pit the two of us against each other. "Your brother practiced piano for an hour today; how much have you practiced today?" Mom would say. "Your sister got an A in this class when she was in the same grade, what did you get?" she would ask. Each time she already knew the answer. Sometimes we would try to be better than each other, but most times we just learned to resent each other's achievements, knowing that Mom would torture us with it later.

My brother was clever. He tested higher than me on IQ tests and exercised his intelligence to accommodate for his laziness. This was first really shown in kindergarten where Mom had already taught him to read quite well but he showed up to class and insisted on not knowing how to read at all. After a few months of this act the concerned kindergarten teacher called Mom in to ask if she could assist in teaching my brother to read. The reality was that my brother had realized quickly that if he played dumb, he received easier homework. His mistake was in not showing enough fake progress to the teacher, leading her to believe he had learning disabilities. Mom hauled him in front of his teacher and forced him to read a paragraph and the stunned teacher then realized she had been fooled this whole time.

A couple times my brother applied the evil genius side of him to get ahead or to try and hurt me. He discovered where the power switches were and which switches were for my room. At the tender age of 7 he found that he could wait until I was a well into doing homework on the computer and then flip the power switch and kill the power to my room. At the time computers were not nearly as good at retaining autosaves and backups. If I hadn't saved any time recently, this could set me all the way back to zero. He knew this would at the very least really bother me and possibly even let him get ahead grade-wise if I really couldn't redo all the work in time. Mom and Dad frowned upon these kinds of tactics and did their best to stop it while I learned to save my work often.

Mom and Dad never let me forget that I was not as naturally gifted as my brother so I worked very hard in my schoolwork. I knew that once my grades were in, I wouldn't have a chance to improve those grades again, so I made sure to put in my best effort. On the other side, my brother always knew the length of the stick he was being measured up against. If I did too well and he felt that the bar was too high, he would feel overwhelmed and hopeless. He began to be less and less motivated to try his best. I don't believe it was fair or good to pit us against each other like this because as the older sibling, I was naturally going to be better, faster, and stronger. However, Mom and Dad continued to use this parenting strategy even into our adult years for all academics, skills, and aspects of life.

* * *

WHEN MY BROTHER REACHED high school, he began binge drinking. Dad often was gifted expensive wines or whiskey or Chinese Baijiu from various work-related people. Dad wasn't much of a drinker though, so he kept it all in the basement. I have no memory of him ever bringing up a bottle even when there was something to celebrate. Dad drank for work only. My brother knew of this unguarded stash and went to the basement. He picked out a large bottle of some hard liquor and that's where it started.

Over time I'm not sure what happened to Dad's gift alcohol, maybe my brother drank it all, maybe Dad hid it or locked it away, maybe it was poured out. Whatever the case, my brother started stealing change from Mom and Dad and using it to buy cheap local liquor, foul tasting stuff. He'd drink and drink, taking shot after shot, rapidly becoming drunk. It was about being drunk, not the taste. We found him asleep on the garage floor more than once, or passed out on the floor of the bathroom, his head near the toilet.

He would pass out in the garage because Mom and Dad didn't give out house keys. Throughout my childhood I never had a key to my house. I had a strict curfew and needed to be home by a certain hour. The door was always locked when Mom and Dad were going to bed so if I didn't get home in time, I'd have to wake one of them to get in the house.

No keys meant easy enforcement of this rule. In Dad's ideal world my curfew would have been 6pm, but I argued that was unreasonable. The truth was he wanted me home for all the hours he was home, even if we didn't do anything together or talk even. He just wanted to know all of his family was home. I'd have to talk him around so that he'd let me stay out to 7 or 8pm. We argued about curfew time even in my early 20s.

My brother on the other hand got a hold of an extra garage key, so he could get into the house through the garage door. To reduce the clunky garage door opening and closing sounds as much as possible, he'd click the garage door open just enough that he could roll under the door. After wriggling in, he'd then click the garage door closed. After the focus and coordination needed for that in addition to the copious amount of alcohol he had imbibed, he'd sometimes fall asleep in the garage.

* * *

TO MAKE MATTERS WORSE, around this time my brother also illegally purchased an old, used motorcycle. He had purchased it with an accumulation of stolen change from Mom and Dad. It was illegal because he was underaged, without a motorcycle license, and had purchased a fake license plate to go with it. The vehicle had trouble starting, some metal bits seemed wigglier than they should be, and it generally sounded like it was on its last legs.

My brother's illegal purchase in combination with his growing alcohol addiction made me angry with him. I knew that he rode several times under the influence. It made me mad that he had such blatant disregard for the law, for his safety, the safety of others who rode on that motorcycle with him, and any potential unlucky person driving near him. Yet he was proud of his motorcycle and showed it off to me in secret.

Shortly after he confided in me and divulged that he parked the motorcycle a few blocks away at a friend's house so that Mom and Dad wouldn't know, I promptly went and relayed this to our parents.

I had hoped they would confiscate the bike. I had hoped they would take action. Instead what happened is I earned my brother's deep hatred and mistrust. He felt greatly betrayed. Mom and Dad ranted and raved, yelled, screamed, but ultimately, they didn't take away the motorcycle.

When I confronted them about it, they whined that my brother had threatened to hurt himself if they took it away. Besides, they said, he'd just buy another one, and they couldn't stop him, so it might as well be this one. I prayed that nothing bad would happen while at the same time believing that something bad was bound to happen. I was declared the "bad guy" in this situation. My brother never forgave me.

* * *

A YEAR OR TWO LATER, there was a pretty harsh consequence. My brother had gone to the local village to binge drink Mongolian rice wine, known to be among the strongest spirits. The alcohol content by volume can reach 54-60%. He admitted to it being his first time drinking this particular alcohol and not being sure of how strong it was, but if anything, that made it more fun for him. He got extremely intoxicated with a couple friends there. One of the friends had ridden on his motorcycle with him to the bar and she expected to ride back with him.

Around 2-3 am, bar was closing and they decided to head home. My brother only had one helmet so he gave it to his passenger and they got on the motorcycle. Before even making it a full block away from the bar, my brother was so drunk that he crashed them into a parked white van. The impact was enough to fling both him and his passenger off the motorcycle. It just so happened that the white van's brake light glass was broken and his face collided into it. The resulting cut was deep and disfiguring. It cut his cheek open and you could see his teeth. It was horrifying.

Mom and Dad were asleep in bed when they got the frantic call from the other drinking friend who had still been waving goodbye from the bar when he saw the crash happen. Between the alcohol and the collision my brother was unresponsive. His passenger had, luckily for her, landed on top of him and was shaken but largely unharmed.

Mom and Dad rushed to where my brother lay in the street and loaded him into their SUV. Despite seeing the blood and being in a panicked mode, they were worried that an ambulance would take him to a local hospital instead of a special surgeon. After seeing his injuries, they were terrified of heavy stitching that could leave him with an unsightly and large facial scar, which could in turn ruin his marriage prospects and in so doing ruin his life. They started looking up numbers and calling up the best plastic/facial surgeons who they felt would be able to use fine stitches and minimize scarring at this hour of the night. Dad's connections came into play here and they were miraculously able to get a facial reconstruction surgeon despite the unreasonable hour of night.

My brother still has a large, crescent scar on his face. Originally it was puckered and angry looking, but eventually it calmed down a little, darkened, and has settled into a permanent scar. Also, originally my brother was quite upset about his "ruined" looks, but over time he felt that it fit with his "bad boy" kind of charm and it actually attracted a lot of girls to him, so he stopped disliking it. Mom and Dad have expressed repeatedly that, if necessary, they can find another plastic surgeon who can perhaps further fix that scar so that it's less obvious but my brother has rejected these offers.

When he awoke in the hospital after the stitching, my brother did swear repeatedly to Mom and Dad that he would never drink again. They were so happy to hear that and they shared it with me. I rolled my eyes while listening to them babble. I felt that my brother was just saying that in light of his condition and that as soon as he was back to his usual health, the drinking would return.

Sure enough, despite the hospital scare and the totaled motorcycle, several months later my brother had a motorcycle again and was back to his drinking habit. I felt sick and tired and helpless.

* * *

AROUND THIS TIME, he also picked up smoking. He'd always felt it was a cool thing to do and being the "bad boy" at school made him popular. He smoked a little and then he started smoking a lot. Mom thought that highlighting the possibility of lung cancer or how smelly he was would stop or slow him. It didn't. She would even hand gather all the cigarette butts he left on the balcony and store them in a jar. The large glass jar displayed how much he had smoked, but that didn't seem to change his habit either. He smoked and drank how much he wanted when he wanted. Mom and Dad seemed to have lost all control over him.

My brother would throw huge tantrums, destroying things, cursing at Mom and Dad if they tried to discipline him in anyway. If pushed too hard he would threaten self-harm or even suicide, which caused Mom and Dad to back off hurriedly. They would be upset and sometimes I caught them crying over my brother's threats. I was not so affected because I didn't believe my brother was capable of doing any significant damage after hearing what the threats were in particular.

One time, my brother threatened to bash his head at the dry wall until Mom and Dad left him alone and stopped asking him to meet his academic obligations. He said he would bash his head until he had brain damage. Mom kept begging and pleading and was very distraught. My reaction, which I did not voice, was an intense desire to get a camera to see if he would follow through with his words. I was certain the most he would manage was perhaps a slight bruise and the wall would be just fine. His head would be just fine as well. And maybe going viral on the internet would show him just how stupid this was. Since Mom caved, my brother ended up not having to hit the wall.

In the end, my brother skipped so many classes that the school asked him to voluntarily leave the school so that they didn't have to put a big fat "expelled" on his academic record. He had skipped more than double the allowed number of missed classes in order to count as a student. Mom and Dad had no choice but to put him in another school and hope that he could get a high school degree.

The distance between my brother and I grew and grew. My parents and I were united in disliking his poor life choices but we could not disagree more on what to do about it. I continued to vocalize to him and my parents my condemnation of what was going on. When I complained to Mom and Dad, they would just throw up their hands and say, "What would you have me do?", "Nothing is working", "He'll just hurt himself", "It's just pushing him to smoke and drink more", and "We have to let him be". I felt that Mom and Dad had given up on him and that was unacceptable.

I was the only one that could discipline him at this time it seemed. I'd be able to insist through tantrums of my own about how he must not smoke in the house. I'd yell about how smelly and terrible it was. It made me sick emotionally and physically when he smoked inside his room. Seeing as this was after I had ended my relationship with Yi, the smell of smoke strongly triggered me. Our rooms were connected through a shared bathroom, so that as the smoke filled his room, it infected my room as well.

My sheets and pillows would smell like smoke. After yelling at him repeatedly, he would reluctantly go smoke on the balcony, which was more than my parents were able to accomplish even though they too hated the smell of smoke. I reasoned with my brother that since I was only home for summer and winter break while I was in college, he would only have to smoke outside for this period of time, after that he could return to his ways.

Summers were hot and winters were cold so sometimes he'd try to bullshit me by putting a fan next to him so that even though it blew the cigarette out sooner he'd at least be able to smoke at his computer desk instead of taking a few steps out to the connected balcony.

I criticized Mom and Dad, blaming them at least partially for my brother's behavior. To defend themselves, they would point to my successes and justify their parenting choices based on how well I had done in school. They laid all the blame on my brother. Our family unit ripped further and further apart.

Mom and Dad did notice the small measure of success I had in getting him to not smoke in the house. Inspired by my example they decided to copy me behind my back. They'd scold him, "Your sister thinks you should go to bed earlier", "your sister thinks your grades aren't good enough", and so on to discipline him. They did not tell me they were using me in this way.

I guess they didn't want him to hate them, so making me the bad guy was the easier way of doing things. By the time I realized what my parents had done, it was too late. My brother truly believed all the terrible things my parents had used me to say. He never believed me when I denied memory of stating the things I was accused of saying or doing. It didn't help my case that Mom and Dad had woven together truth with lies and some of the fabrications they came up with were not entirely farfetched.

By the time I completed college, we were barely on speaking terms.

25

Although there were struggles throughout my childhood, the last semester of high school was definitely the hardest. There was my brother and his smoking and drinking and fights related to that, there was Mom and Dad fighting with me over Yi, and there was fighting over college Mom and Dad fighting with me over my choices and fighting over my future.

Mom and Dad argued fiercely over what I should be or what I was good at. I felt like Dad took a more active role in parenting for the first time, like it was suddenly dawning on him how close I was to becoming an adult. I think he thought he still had more time before I'd grown up and was going to fly the coop so to speak.

So, Dad advised me on the only thing he knew; his own path to success. Dad had been a mechanical engineer originally, and eventually got his degree in petroleum engineering to go work in big oil. He experienced a lot of stability, great salary, great perks for him and our family, and a fulfilling career. It made sense that he wanted me to follow exactly in his footsteps. He didn't know any other path, so he didn't understand why I'd want to reject that certainty and do something unknown.

I wasn't sure what I wanted to do or to be. Up to this point I'd had precious little thoughts of my own about my future. School's limited curriculum largely dictated the courses I took, Mom dictated the rest of my life from extracurriculars to what I wore. I'd never even decorated my room growing up. She made all the choices, even telling me what to feel.

I didn't know what to do. How was I to choose this major decision for my future when I had no idea what the implications were, or what life would be like in college or after. I only had my past experiences to pull from. In my mind, I guessed college to just be a little harder than high school and that I'd be living away from the home, which in and of itself was already difficult enough to imagine.

Mom wanted me to be a doctor. She thought the family would greatly benefit from having a doctor in the family. They might have suggested a lawyer or something affiliated with the government, but they decided that our family had less to gain from the perks of having a family member in these positions. Health was definitely a top concern of Mom's, possibly influenced by grandma's health concerns and the fact that two of my grandparents had passed away recently to different forms of cancer.

Dad and Mom went back and forth on this subject. Sometimes the arguments they had would escalate to shouting. Their arguing and anxiety about looming deadlines for when I had to submit these applications finally pushed me to take one of my first steps about making a major decision in my life.

I stood up in the middle of the shouting and suggested an in-between option. I could be a biomedical engineer. It meant that after completing my degree in 4 years I would again have the option of choosing between engineering vs medical field. I knew that I was just kicking the ball a little further down the road. I knew this debate would come up again, but right now I needed time and less conflict. There was already plenty of shouting in the house, this was just one topic of shouting that I had some small power over and I could make it stop. And it stopped.

Peace restored, Mom and Dad went about choosing a list of schools for me to apply to and then had me write essays and applications to each. Dad's heavy attachment to Northwestern University meant that he forced me to apply there as an Early Decision applicant. Early Decision applications are binding—a student accepted as an Early Decision applicant would have to attend that college. My hands would be tied. I did not want this. I did not want to be Dad. I did not want this life. I also didn't want Dad visiting me and Northwestern was in Chicago, a major flight hub that Dad flew to all the time. Mom and Dad would hate me for it but I wanted to find my own path in life.

I hated being forced into applying Early Decision. I hated having to write every single forced essay and filling every forced application to a list of colleges chosen for me by Mom and Dad. In their graciousness, they did allow me to select one school independent of their list. In a vicious mood, I asked dad where his boss' boss had graduated from. He had often admired the wealth and success of his boss' boss aloud at home. Grudgingly Dad said his superior had graduated from Vanderbilt University, so that was the school I added as the last school on the list.

I tried my best to write a terrible essay to Northwestern that would guarantee my rejection, but it had to still be good enough to pass Mom and Dad's watchful eyes. They checked every essay and application I sent so I couldn't sabotage it too obviously. I crossed my fingers and waited anxiously, hoping for rejection after I sent everything off.

The following months felt like years as I waited for the admission decisions to be sent back to us. I prayed that Northwestern would reject me and that Vanderbilt would accept me. It was agony. Even if Vanderbilt accepted me, I could still be forced to go to Northwestern. And even then, any school that accepted me was accepting me as a biomedical engineer major. A major that I had no passion for and no idea what that future could be like. Everything felt hopeless, but at least, going to college meant that I might have more hope and freedom than staying at home.

The first decision to come back was the Early Decision. Northwestern rejected me. Hallelujah! I wanted to celebrate but I had to act just as devastated as Dad looked. I felt a small sense of achievement. Dad was furious, angry, and deeply disappointed. He was convinced that my future was going to be a disaster now. He ranted and raved and threw insults at me. Looking back, I'm sure he felt lost about what my life was going to be like and felt he was losing control over my future and that made him feel desperation and despair.

Unfortunately, several other schools rejected me as well, and I began to feel some anxiety. Somehow though, not all of them rejected me and one of the few that did accept me was Vanderbilt University. I announced that I wished to go to this school.

Dad wasn't at all happy with this idea. Vanderbilt was in Nashville, Tennessee, a city he had never been to and in which he had no contacts. His meticulous planning required for me to be accepted to Northwestern University, so that he could have asked his friends there to keep a watchful eye on me and he could swing by relatively often during his business trips in America.

I breathed a sigh of relief. The future seemed bright again.

26

When my flight to college was only a month away, Yi asked if I would marry him. It wasn't a proposal, only a discussion. He wanted to buy me a promise ring. I suppose it was an attempt to keep our relationship going in light of the huge time difference and physical distance that would be between us once I was overseas. I expressed my reservations and so he didn't fight too hard when I broke up with him a couple of months later from America.

My family flew with me to the US to drop me off. Together, we shopped for anything and everything we/they thought I could use. My dorm room filled up with stuff. I had a room at the end of the hall next to the fire escape all to myself. It was so far down the hallway that at night, the hall light didn't quite reach my door. It was almost as if I didn't exist. I loved it!

Mom and Dad were very worried about how easily I might be distracted at college with all the newness of everything. They warned me over and over to not make friends and to focus on my studies. They stressed that I shouldn't join any student clubs or organizations, but to focus on the classes, don't fall behind, and stay safe.

They set me up with a phone plan and phone tracking app so that they could see my location at all times. Dad enjoyed texting me about my little blue blip blinking away on his phone as I went from class to dorm and back again. He loved the convenience of the app, which let him call me the moment I was back in my room.

In a few short days, Mom had us wrestle the room into working order. She fretted about where the bed or desk should be and had us arrange and rearrange several times until she was satisfied.

Right as we were finishing up, it was time for me to go to the pre-orientation program. I remember how Mom's eyes filled with tears as I strode away from her in the lobby. The lobby filled with parents of all these hundreds of freshmen who were starting on their college journey. There were tearful farewells everywhere, but I felt so excited and happy that I could barely contain myself. Mom sensed this, I think, and after dragging me into an awkward hug (since we so rarely hugged) she let me go.

I hustled towards the doors into the room where the freshmen were being organized. I held tightly onto the program folder that I had been given so that I could read about where we were going.

I didn't turn back, and Mom never let me forget it. She told me she cried bitterly all the way back to the hotel that her dear daughter marched away after an unsatisfactory goodbye and didn't turn back once. In fights years later, she would bring up this memory and how much it hurt her that her daughter was an emotionless monster.

27

The pre-orientation program was not quite what I expected. On paper, the pictures showed that it would be at a kind of camp location with a lake. There was a wooden house where the faculty would sleep, but the rest of us were divided into groups of about ten kids with various student leaders and we would be sleeping in tents. Our student leader was a short sophomore guy with a good tan. He described himself as knowing all the ins and outs of college life, and promised to teach us all we needed to know. Being naive and eager to learn as much as we could, we followed him without question to the area where we would be camping so that we could place our backpacks down.

Under the best of circumstances, I had never been into camping. I didn't enjoy the feeling of treading on crunchy leaves and snapping twigs; I didn't like thinking about the system of roots and bugs and whatever else that lay under our feet. Lying down was worse, the sleeping bag and tent would offer minimal padding and the ground would still be uncomfortable to lie on and try to sleep. I was even less excited at the prospect of being jammed into dinky, smelly, used tents with a bunch of strangers.

After we reached the camping spot, our sophomore leader assured us our stuff would be safe and instructed us to unpack and set up the tents.

There were five girls, five boys, and our student leader in our group. Although the student leader already knew this, it was a huge shock to the group that there were only three tents. Us girls seemed more dismayed. One tent was meant to protect our backpacks/luggage, one tent could fit up to 3 people, and one large tent was meant for the rest of us to squeeze in.

Three of the girls either already knew each other or just bonded immediately and so, before us two remaining girls could figure it out, they decided the three of them were taking the small tent, which they promptly nicknamed the "princess tent". That left me and one other girl. The other girl snapped out of shock faster than I did, and claimed the corner spot, which meant my body would be squashed between her and the males.

I was horrified. Even if it weren't for my experiences with Yi, physical touch in general with anyone of either sex was a foreign concept to me. I had not grown up being all touchy and feely and definitely was not comfortable with such close proximity with strangers. I felt sick, and yet, I also wanted desperately to fit in and not draw attention. As much as the corner girl didn't relish the idea, she did not appear to be in as much distress as I was experiencing on the inside. I did my best to put on a brave face and stuffed all my emotions down.

I tried to numb myself as we trudged to the open area where the professor leading the program would give us a speech. We listened to a rundown of the activities we would complete in the next couple of days. With so many freshmen at the camp, we would be rotating to different activity stations; playing in the lake, hiking in the woods, playing at the pool—that sort of thing. The faculty leader ended with safety instructions and – in a surprisingly joking tone—mentioned that there was to be no "baby-making". This led to titters of laughter from the students. It took me a full extra minute to realize what he meant. I had not even considered sex to be a possibility. All my fear was suddenly brought up again, and I struggled to breathe evenly so that no one could see that I was on the verge of a major breakdown.

One of the first activities in my group required us to be in our bathing suits. I felt awkward and uncomfortable with being around so many people and not fully clothed. We scampered without shoes over to where we stood in line to be flung into the lake on a bouncy blob. One person would be sitting at one end of the blob and another would jump off the tower to bounce them high into the air and into the lake. The blob bounce looked like a lot of fun, but the walk to the wooden jumping tower was brutal on my soft, bare feet. I'd almost never walked without socks and shoes. I struggled with each step.

Our student leader took pity on my limping and wincing form and let me wear his flip flops. His feet were much tougher from often walking barefoot, he said. Although immensely grateful at his kindness, this created a new kind of challenge for me. His flip flops were too big and I was confused at this footwear. I had never worn flip flops. They produced a new kind of agony. The rope that was meant to be between my toes cut into the flesh and it was extremely painful, so much so that I could not wear them properly. Instead, I squeezed my toes together to block the rope and shuffled awkwardly the entire way to the tower, scooting the flip flops by kicking them along the ground under my feet.

After reaching the front of the queue, I quickly forgot about how awful the walking had been. Bouncing onto the blob was a lot of fun and I whooped happily when I was launched into the air.

For the next activity, we combined several of the student groups. We were to play icebreaker games which included a game much like "musical chairs". In this game, music played while students walked around the room. As soon as the music stopped, the speaker would call out a command. Depending on what he shouted, players would have to rapidly find a partner and pick them up, or hug them, or something. As a result, as the music played, the boys would hound the girls closely, to be ready to snatch them up for whatever command was called.

I was terrified. After watching the boys pounce on the girls and swoop them up in their arms from the sidelines while my group waited it for our turn to play, I looked around desperately to see what other people thought.

To my surprise, no one voiced a complaint and everyone seemed to be enjoying the game. I felt alone. Maybe I was the only one who had anything against the game. Maybe I was the weird one for not liking it.

My group was called, and I shuffled unhappily into the play zone. Luckily, the first couple of rounds didn't include the "pick up" command and so I stayed in the game until the command to "PICK UP!" was shouted out. I saw one of the guys rushing towards me, but I immediately went so entirely limp that when he reached me, I had already collapsed before he could pick me up. He was bitterly disappointed and stomped away. I wasn't sure if it was more because it meant we were both eliminated from the round, or because he didn't get to pick me up. Whatever the case, I quickly retreated to the sidelines again where other people had already lost and moved far away from the guy who had tried to pick me up. I didn't look at him.

My nerves were on the brink of shattering when we went to the next activity. I prayed that since the sun was setting, it was going to be something less stressful. I breathed a sigh of relief when our leader told us that this would be an easier game. He informed us that we would be "spooning". I hadn't heard of this term before, and did not know what it meant, but I didn't want to look like a fool by asking a stupid question.

Everyone else seemed to already know what the word meant. I figured I would wait for him to describe it in more detail and that I'd be able to piece together this new word from that context. He declared that he was known as the "Spoon King" and another student group leader backed him up on this claim. He and the other student leader giggled as they paired us off by numbering us with ones and twos.

At first, our leader pronounced that we would spoon in partners, and later he had us spoon in a giant circle of spooning people lying on the ground. He explained he'd blow on a whistle for us to change partners but that we would essentially be spooning with whomever our partner was for a couple minutes before moving on to the next person. Almost everyone was giggling and looked eager to engage in this activity. When I finally understood that spooning meant two people lying closely together, and that girls had purposefully been paired with boys, I wanted to faint.

I could not understand why everyone was so happy. Maybe if I were a normal person, if I were just like them, I would be looking forward to this, too? When I looked around, I could see the professors and faculty members chuckling as they watched us play the icebreaker games and the spooning game.

Since they weren't stepping in to stop anything and if anything seemed merely amusing, I thought I was the only one who wasn't comfortable. I thought it would be wrong for me to say something to the contrary. I thought back to conversations with Yi. Maybe I was supposed to like these kinds of activities.

But I wasn't like them, and I was shaking so badly and could barely hide my tears when my first spoon partner approached me, that he gave me some space and looked eager to move on from me—the weirdo girl who was having a full-blown panic attack at this point. I felt awful and miserable and alone.

Another student group leader—a girl—noticed my distress and took pity on me, claiming me as her spoon partner for the rest of this activity and simply lay quietly next to me while I regained control over my emotions.

Finally, the day was over. I was exhausted and ready to crash when our group trudged back to our campsite. Then I remembered that we were supposed to squeeze together in the large tent. I obediently stepped into the tent and tried my best to lie there in my corner of the tent while the guys squeezed in. We couldn't all lie in a row, so one person had to lie in the area that blocked the exit of the tent. I felt trapped and claustrophobic.

My heartbeat was fast from panic and discomfort. I couldn't breathe, and the tent was rapidly growing stuffy. There was no way I could fall asleep, but I was so tired that I just lay there with my eyes wide open. I could hear some of the guys snoring and the quiet breathing of the girl lying next to me. Her breath was even but I wondered if she too struggled to sleep in this situation.

Deciding that between the horrifying proximity to all the guys, the sound of all the snoring, and the stuffy heat in the tent was too much for me to overcome, I quietly gathered my sleeping bag and stepped over the guy in the tent's doorway area to get out. Outside was much cooler, and I felt better immediately. I didn't inform anyone where I was going, and no one asked.

I took my sleeping bag and started trudging towards where the common area had been where we had been asked to form the spoon circle. I remembered that the faculty's wood house was there, as well as some giant lights that lit up the field in front. I decided that would be a safe location, so I laid out my sleeping bag and slept there in the grass, under the huge light, in full view of the front door of the wood house. I slept peacefully, trusting university rules and staff would protect me.

28

The pre-orientation program ended and we were shuttled back to the on-campus dorms. I loved my dorm room. It was a tiny little thing where I had to loft the bed so that the dresser could fit underneath and still have enough floor space left for a desk. I'd vault awkwardly into bed every night. I picked pink and green watermelon colors for my bedding, since I loved watermelon so much. Just looking at the color pattern reminded me of the cool, sweet fruit. It was comforting.

I'd never been involved in decorating my room before. Mom always chose the furniture and anything on the walls according to what she believed was best. In recent years, she had been obsessed with her antique Chinese furniture with warped handles and old wood. Prior to her Chinese furniture preference, Mom had me use some baby pink furniture, which Mom thought was girly and hoped that it would have an effect on me. Unfortunately for her, I still cared nothing about my looks or about other supposedly girly things. Now that I had my own room, and Mom was an ocean away from me, I could do what I liked with it, so I did just that.

One of the first things I did, was pepper my walls with various posters. Some were of flowers, landscapes, or animals. Some were optical illusions, because I thought they were cool, and others were just random images I'd found while plowing through the poster section in various stores. Lying in bed, I could turn and see all my favorite things around me. I was happy.

Freedom was intoxicating. I didn't know what came after college—what life was supposed to be like or where I would be going—but I knew I couldn't go back to how my life had been at home. I couldn't imagine living without freedom now that I'd had a taste of living with it.

* * *

ALONG WITH THE FREEDOM, there was a ton to learn when I first arrived at college. It was only after Mom and Dad had officially dropped me off and boarded the plane back to China that I realized I had not been taught any survival or daily life skills. Sure, I knew how to brush my teeth and wash myself, but I had not been taught to do laundry, to fold it up, or even to tie my laces right. I had rarely handled money, did not know anything about paying bills or budgeting, or how to order food on my own at a restaurant.

The first time I had to do laundry, I carried my dirty clothes down to the laundry room in a basket. The room was quiet and no washers or dryers were running. I plopped onto one of the machines, and waited. And waited. Until someone else came into the laundry room, as I had, with a basket of dirty clothes. I tried not to stare too obviously, but I watched them pop some coins into the slot and push them in with the little metal lever, then select the settings they wanted, and leave. Several minutes after they had left their clothes, I puttered over to the machine they had used that was now rumbling away. Curiously, I looked at the settings that the dial was on, and made sure I copied their exact selections.

Since the other person had used the warm setting, I used it too. They selected normal, so I selected normal as well. In observing others in the laundry room, or trying to bring it up casually in conversation with people, I learned over time about the other settings. I had a hard time choosing laundry settings because, unlike clothing sold in America, my clothing purchased in China did not have tags indicating their washing settings.

Similarly, for other "adulting" things, I learned on my own through experience or by mimicking others. I would try to casually ask how often someone washed their bedding for example. I often felt embarrassed or ashamed of not knowing things that other people seemed to already know. I at least slightly resented Mom and Dad for not doing much in the way of preparing me for these important life skills. Nonetheless, one bit at a time, I learned how to live on my own.

29

Unsurprisingly, my first semester at Vanderbilt was pretty rough. My feelings of self-worth were essentially that, as long I was still worthy of being fucked or raped, then I still deserved to be in this world.

I was never considered to be good-looking or above average as far as I was concerned all throughout school. I'm told I was a cute kid, but there's a lot of cute kids. I was never pursued in middle or high school as one of the hot girls or cute girls, which didn't bother me at all since I was not interested in being pursued. Somewhat surprisingly, I didn't have any body image issues. I felt that I was plain and average, and that was fine by me.

When I came to the US, there was a change though. Nashville didn't have a lot of Asians, let alone young Asian girls. All of a sudden, I became an exotic animal, sexualized based solely on race. Also, in freshman year, many freshmen were interested in exploring sex. I was told that upperclassmen were particularly more interested in dating new freshman girls. Almost immediately, there was a lot of attention, lots of glances and words, invitations, and pressure to date or have sex. It terrified and horrified me.

I couldn't understand why anyone was interested in this activity, since I didn't have any interest in it at all. Whenever someone expressed physical or romantic interest in me in any way, it felt as though I was being held at gunpoint. I would try to be polite and remain in control when I was in public. At first opportunity I would flee to the safety and isolation of my dorm room and cry or be sick. Because, for me, the only sex I had experienced was with Yi, and all I knew was his version of sex—which was rape. Therefore, in my mind, all these boys wanted to rape me.

I had flown over to the other side of the world to escape Yi and the life I had left behind, and yet here it was again, waiting for me and in far greater numbers. I was so sick and afraid, I wanted to die. I wanted to make it stop, because I felt the walls closing in on me. So, I hatched a desperate—and perhaps stupid—plan.

30

I chose someone, one of the boys. I had no feelings for him, but he seemed like a safe pick. His name was Luke. He seemed to be a harmless philosophy major. Luke was the scrawny and weak type who never worked out. Though only 18 years old, from poor sitting and standing posture, he seemed permanently somewhat hunched. He lacked confidence and aggression, which made me feel that it would be unlikely for him to dominate me as Yi had. Most importantly, he was still a virgin. I was so confident and ignorant about guys that I thought this meant he would be less likely to have an interest in sex.

I was very frank and told him that I needed protection. I wanted to put up an act, go with him to public events and hold his hand on the way to class; I wanted to eat with him in the cafeteria as if I were a girlfriend. I prayed that other guys would back off if it looked like I was in a relationship. I remembered that other guys had left me alone when I was with Yi. Luke agreed without resistance and we acted accordingly.

My plan appeared to be working. After I informed anyone pursuing me that I was with Luke, they stopped asking me to date them.

* * *

OVER TIME, HE SHARED that he was actually very interested in having sex with me. I felt a corner of my heart break. Maybe this was life and I needed to learn to cope with it. Everyone seemed to want this.

I shared with Luke my reservations and a bit about my prior experiences with Yi. I think a small part of me hoped that knowing I was damaged in this way would reduce his interest. Maybe he would stop wanting sex with me. Surely, anyone with an ounce of empathy would not make me do this thing.

It didn't. He successfully pressured me into having sex with him. I found myself in this dark place again; this place where I did not want to be. I did not want to engage in this activity. But I was still not educated on the concept of rape and the concept of consent. Besides, months of conditioning made it impossible for me to resist physically anymore, although I doubted I would have been able to fight him off anyways. I had already failed so many times in this struggle before. I had already accepted that I was always going to lose this fight. My confused mind couldn't understand why this was happening again. What was the point of being here? How could I have been so wrong about Luke? Coming to the US was supposed to be happiness and freedom, at least from this.

[Why.]

I'd cry sometimes before and after sex; I'd cry and ask him to stop during the act. I'd beg—*please!*—But my voice was weak, my pleas weaker; easy to ignore, easy to forget.

Maybe that's why he didn't care. I blamed myself often.

Occasionally, he would feel guilty and mutter that he wouldn't ask for it again, but a few days would pass, and he would do it again. I wasn't sure what to do. But if it were between fending off several people who wanted to have sex with me versus letting Luke have his way, I thought it was still safer and less painful to stay with Luke.

31

I had nightmares almost every night. I'd wake up exhausted and reeling from the violence I witnessed or experienced in my dreams. During the day, I developed paranoia that Yi would come and find me and make me his again.

In my sleep, I'd dream I was being pursued and hunted until I was caught and killed or that I took my own life. That seemed to be the only way to escape the nightmares when I was in my dream. I tried to numb myself, but there was too much pain, and I started to lose control. I began having frequent panic attacks. Sometimes, when I closed my eyes, I could hear myself screaming.

Panic attacks are terrible. I'm not sure how others experience them, but for me, it meant that I would be curled up in the fetal position, shuddering and hyperventilating with my eyes squeezed shut. If someone tried to comfort me and moved my arm or shifted my head, I would scream at their touch.

Sometimes, I would cry during these panic attacks. I would hyperventilate so violently that my body hurt. Usually, I wouldn't be able to talk during a panic attack. If I did, I didn't make much sense. I'd repeat apologies that I had repeated in the past that hadn't stopped the past from happening, but I repeated them desperately as though they could.

32

There were many student clubs at Vanderbilt. Often, there were performances or events on campus. I would occasionally attend an event just to see what was out there. One of the clubs was called "Spoken Word", something I had never heard of before.

For their performance, they spoke passionately about various Vanderbilt and college-related statistics. This was when I first learned the meaning of the word "rape" and the importance of consent. In their speech, they talked about the high rate at which students experienced sexual harassment, assault, and/or rape; the figures were supposedly one in four.

I learned that there were organizations that victims could report assaults to and from which they could receive protection. They encouraged students who wished to speak about the wrongs of the world to join them in writing and performing poetry. Unwittingly, this spoken poem was what educated me on the topic. I sat in the audience stunned. I had not known I was a victim. This profoundly changed how I thought about Yi and Luke.

Now that I knew what rape was, all the wrongs that had happened to me, became clear. Much of my confusion was cleared away. However, by truly understanding what had happened with Yi and Luke, I felt intense emotional pain cut into me. When I didn't have a name for it and didn't know what it was or that it was wrong, it hadn't hurt me so much. Now I knew that there was a world out there where three out of four people lived without experiencing rape, without experiencing abuse. I knew that there were organizations to which those who did experience these atrocities could report to, and they would be protected. I wanted to be a part of that world.

Luke saw my distress, but he was benefiting from the months of conditioning that Yi had invested in me. The careful, painful lessons Yi had instilled in me so that I would behave and do everything correctly and not fight back.

33

Luke wasn't completely without compassion and he held up his end of the bargain for the most part. We held hands at public events, ate together in the cafeteria, and shared the same group of friends. He'd hold me when I cried about my nightmares or memories, he'd console me and shield me from some of that pain. He accompanied me sometimes to classes and encouraged me in my hobbies. We took pictures together like couples, and it was nice to play pretend, nice to have company. Luke patiently listened to me chatter about anything and everything. And despite that I had initiated this relationship based solely on needing protection, I felt myself strangely begin to like him for more than just that.

Sometimes when Luke promised he wouldn't ask me to do things that made me cry anymore, he seemed to believe it himself. He did feel bad, and he had a lot of internal conflict, but he wanted sex badly. Watching me convulse into panic attacks afterwards or tearfully beg him to stop only slightly deterred him.

I struggled with coming to terms about what to do about Luke and how to think about him. I began dissociating, disconnecting whenever he wanted to fuck me. I experienced frequent episodes of amnesia as my brain tried to protect me with deleting upsetting memories.

Losing track of hours at a time scared me badly. I considered leaving Luke but I was too afraid of being alone. I felt I needed his arms around me when I was having panic attacks. I desperately needed him just as I had needed Yi.

I remembered what the "Spoken Word" performance had mentioned. How it was important to talk to friends and family. Family was out of the question, so I tried to confide in my new freshmen friends what was going on with me and Luke.

The definition of rape is "the penetration, no matter how slight, of the vagina or anus with any body part or object, or oral penetration by a sex organ of another person, without the consent of the victim". So that's the word I used. Rape. It was still rape, even though I didn't fight him physically, right? Still rape, since I didn't want it and let him know with my words, my begging, my tears.

My friends didn't believe me. Luke didn't look like a rapist or an abuser to them. To them, Luke was just the goofy, nerdy philosophy major. I was told to stop being crazy and talking about Luke in a negative way, since it wasn't true. It was that, or be cast out from the group.

I stopped talking about it. My panic attacks increased in frequency, sometimes happening several times a day. I lost my appetite, lost weight, and lost the motivation to attend classes. I started going to classes later and later, and eventually, started skipping them entirely.

I was already falling apart when Luke delivered the final blow. One day after class he asked to talk to me. He confessed that our relationship was entirely about the sex, at least for him, and if we couldn't do that without him feeling guilty, then this really just wasn't what he wanted. He apologized for using my body for sex and he even shed a few tears that seemed genuine.

I stared blankly ahead. Inside, I felt like a bomb had gone off and blown my whole world apart. The only thing that gave me value in the world, was now being taken away. I wasn't even worth the sex anymore. I truly was worthless.

I went to my room. I cried and wondered what I should do now. I was working on a major I hated, to go towards a life just like Dad's— which I didn't find appealing— and the only present value that I had, which was to be used for sex, had just been taken from me. I had no compelling future and I was waste of existence in the present. I had no close bonds with the other freshmen, and no one who believed me. I had no childhood friends from my past—just a family that I did not feel supported by who were an ocean away. I had nowhere to turn, nowhere to go, and nothing to work towards. It was a recipe for disaster.

34

A couple months prior to this breakup, on a group trip to the grocery store, we saw that there was an enormous bottle of painkillers, the biggest bottle any of us had ever seen. Luke had intended to purchase a bottle of painkillers anyways, and purchased this unnecessarily large one for the silliness of its size. I wondered now how many painkillers were in that bottle—how many hundreds?

I stopped crying when I remembered this bottle. Suddenly, I was filled with purpose and determination. I didn't know how many painkillers it took to die, but I was going to find out.

I knew that when Luke was in class, he often didn't lock his door. I ran down the stairs and yanked open the stiff wooden drawer in which he kept them. I took the bottle, closed the drawer, and went back to my room. I snatched a mug and went down the hall to fill it with water, before I sat down with my water and the massive bottle of painkillers. I looked around my room.

My room; the first time I'd really felt remotely close to owning anything. Prior to this, everything had been Mom and Dad's. College life had been my greatest hope. I closed my eyes. I had failed to find happiness despite having travelled so far. And the one thing that had given me a sense of worth, was now no longer in existence.

I didn't know what to do. I was terrified of what would happen if word got out that Luke no longer wanted me. That would invite attention from the other hungry, sex-motivated guys. If Luke was one of the more harmless ones, who knew what waited for me?

I shook in horror. I couldn't do it again; I wouldn't do it again. And I still had one thing left that I had control over. Even if I could control little else in my life, at least I had control over ending it.

I popped open the bottle, which was filled with little red pills. "Extra strength", the label read. Maybe that would mean I wouldn't have to swallow quite so many of them.

I swiftly poured a handful out onto my palm as if they were popcorn kernels. I didn't count; I just pushed them into my mouth and gulped some water to make them go down. I repeated that until I couldn't bear the taste of the pills anymore.

Then, I put the bottle on the dresser and lay down on my bed, staring at the ceiling. I had a poster on the ceiling too; it was an optical image of stairs that kept going into each other, never leading out of themselves. When I had first purchased this poster, I had liked it. But now it seemed to be mocking me. I had thought I'd found a way out, but I was trapped, just like those stairs. And now, the only way out, was these pills.

I shifted onto my side so that I wouldn't be looking at that poster anymore. I laid there and waited for the world to fall away. I closed my eyes and smiled. I was going to be free.

[Free.]

* * *

THE PILLS MUST HAVE kicked in. I felt a tremendous sense of clarity; my senses were heightened, sharpened. My joy became overwhelming, my heart beating fast in anticipation of leaving the world behind. I felt no pain. I felt light.

Then I heard the familiar sound of Luke's door opening and closing. "Luke," I thought, "I should tell Luke. I should let him know I am going away and I am going to be free."

I clawed myself up to sitting position. My muscles were starting to slip away from my control, but I wanted Luke to know how happy I was and how happy I was going to be, forever. I giggled and stumbled my way down the stairs to his room.

He was sitting on his chair and looked surprised when I entered. He was expecting me to still be in tears over his announcement of our "breakup". Yet, here I was, all smiles.

I leaned heavily on the doorframe and closed the door behind me. I asked him how his class had gone, and he talked to me about it as usual. It was as if everything was still the same. He made no move to get up from his chair, and we both chatted comfortably for a little while.

Unable to stand anymore, I sank weakly into his beanbag chair while he rattled on about his day. I doubt he noticed my slow movements, I had already become quite weak over the past several weeks since I hadn't been eating or sleeping much, and he knew this.

There was a brief lull in our conversation, and I blurted out, "Check your desk drawer". He looked at me, confused. "Check your desk drawer," I repeated.

There were only three, and he jerked open the drawer that housed the painkillers last. Staring blankly at it for a moment, he asked quietly what I'd done with his bottle of painkillers. I started cackling, laughing until I coughed.

My throat felt strange and dry from swallowing the pills. He jumped up from his chair and shouted at me, "WHERE ARE THE PAINKILLERS?"

I told him they were on my dresser upstairs in my room, and he left swiftly to retrieve them. He was back in seconds, bottle open and staring at the contents, trying to remember how many painkillers had remained from the last time he'd taken any of the pills. I doubt it occurred to him how determined I had been at consuming them; perhaps he thought I'd only taken a couple. I'd told him before that I rarely took any medication, even painkillers, when I was in pain.

I was still grinning when he started shaking me by my shoulders and demanding that I tell him how much I'd taken. Truthfully, I told him I didn't know. He rushed to the dorm phone; all the rooms were equipped with one so that you could easily dial various campus services or friends' rooms.

I wasn't sure how long it would take before I was past the point of no return, but I figured I might still need to buy a few minutes, so I tried to jump up from my position on the beanbag chair to stop him from dialing the emergency number.

A bad idea; my leg muscles collapsed halfway through the process of standing, and I ended up falling on him. It was enough to jolt the phone out of his hand and delay him.

Pissed off and freaking out, he let me lay on the floor, picked up the phone again, and dialed. I barely felt any of the impact of my fall, but I was angry now, too. How dare he obstruct my happiness?

I was about to be free. I was about to take control of my life. Why could he not let me have this, this one little thing? Please.

But it was too late; he hung up the phone and said that the campus transport was coming to bring me to the college hospital. They would be here in minutes.

Luke wrestled me into a sitting position and even gently brushed the red skin of my cheek that had so recently hit the floor.

He explained that we needed to wait for the transport people out by the front door of our dorm building, and I nodded numbly. I could barely think anymore; my body felt like putty. It couldn't be long now. I must have swallowed nearly a hundred pills. I thought if it would reduce his anxiety in these final moments, I'd cooperate. Surely it shouldn't matter anymore. Surely, it had been long enough for the painkillers in my body to cause irreparable, fatal damage.

Luke awkwardly—but determinedly—dragged me to my feet and together, we lurched and stumbled down the hallway. Two men were jogging up to the door by the time we reached the lobby. Together, the three of them assisted me into their vehicle.

Luke and I sat in the backseat. The brief car ride made me feel sick, which was weird. I was never car sick. Dreamily, I wondered what would happen to me next. I felt no pain, but I was very sleepy.

* * *

I WAS RUSHED INTO a white hospital room. The doctor or nurse attempted to ask me several questions. When was my birthday? What type of pills had I taken? How many? I felt flustered by the rapid-fire questioning and didn't want to cooperate, but Luke was able to answer most of it. After that, they let me lay down in a room and I was alone with Luke again for a moment.

I was falling asleep. I felt very peaceful. Luke started crying and put his head in his hands. I closed my eyes happily, and I slept.

[Goodbye.]

35

When I woke up, I was in another room and Luke was not there. I was alone, but why was I awake? I shouldn't be awake. No, this was not the way it was supposed to be!

Furious, I found that I was in a hospital gown now. Shakily, I tried to stand. I needed to pee and I could see there was a toilet in the corner of the room. There was a sharp pain in my wrist when I moved. Looking down, I saw that I had an IV. I also had one of those heart rate monitors squeezing one of my fingers.

I took off the heart rate monitor and I guess that alerted one of the nurses, who opened the door. She immediately knew what I was trying to do and assisted me over to the toilet. I was ashamed of how weak and very confused I felt.

Doctors and nurses would take turns over the next couple of days coming into my room in the Intensive Care Unit (ICU) to ask me how to contact my parents for insurance information, and to update them on my recovery. I was uncooperative; too upset that I had failed at taking my own life.

The doctors explained how close it had been; how close I came to death—just another couple of minutes would probably have been too late. They mentioned that as if I was supposed to be grateful and pleased, but all I could think about was how I had been such a fool and failed at exerting this one tiny bit of control over my life. Had I been patient and stayed in my bed, I would have succeeded. I wanted to get out of the hospital, but I was so weak.

I eventually caved and told the doctors my parents' information, since I had no way to pay the hospital bills. Mom and Dad were called and informed as to where I was. I'm not sure how they were told. They called me on the phone and raged at me over the hospital bills and roared about how stupid I had been.

I didn't know how to answer them.

I wished I'd died.

***

I SLEPT MOST OF THE TIME. Any movement tired me out horribly. My friends and Luke came to visit briefly between classes, but they were distant and nervous around me. I tried to put on a good face when they were around, but in reality, I wanted to disappear. I didn't want to exist anymore.

A nurse told me that I would be released once my condition was stable, and as standard procedure, I would be moved to a mental care facility to make sure I was no longer suicidal. By mental care facility, they meant psych ward. The health insurance I had through Dad didn't cover staying at the campus hospital's facility, so I had to be moved elsewhere to save money.

Campus transport came to pick me up. The hospital staff led me downstairs and directed me towards the door. A couple of my friends were waiting outside to see me off. They hugged me and I made my way carefully towards the last few steps where the campus transport car was waiting. My legs felt weak, either from still recovering or the anticipated destination, or both.

The driver seemed tense as he explained that he needed to restrain me for safety reasons. I didn't understand. My friends came over and asked that I not be handcuffed. They were roughly shoved away as the cold metal was closed around my wrists behind me, and I was pushed into the car. As the door was closed, I could see my friends crying and raging. I found myself crying, too.

I found that this was highly inconvenient, since, in my seat belted and handcuffed condition, I had no way of wiping my tears or my nose. I also could not sit upright. I leaned forward for the duration of the ride to not put pressure on my hands and wrists, periodically wiping my face quietly on the bone of my knees. It was a long car ride.

36

Upon reaching the mental care facility, I was escorted to a long, narrow, white hallway with white rooms on either side, white beds, white sheets, and staff in white clothing.

As an 18-year-old, the staff had discussed briefly whether I should be placed in the adult ward or the teenage ward. After they had interviewed me, I had been deemed mature enough to be in the adult ward, and so I was the youngest among several inmates. Most of them seemed to be in their 40s or older. A few were clearly out of their mind.

A loud scream caused me to flinch involuntarily as we walked down the hall to my room. There was a lady on the opposite side of the hall to me. She was perched on her sink, screaming at a corner of the ceiling. A nurse explained that this lady thought she was a bird, so she'd "call" or scream randomly.

This would be the first time I experienced therapy. I knew little about mental health therapy or the professionals associated with it. I only knew that Mom and Dad had strongly expressed that they were untrustworthy, expensive, and would sometimes prescribe drugs that would take a month to start having an effect. It all seemed like voodoo magic and a load of crap. And yet, here I was, locked in a hallway of small rooms dedicated to that.

My roommate was a larger lady with scars all over her arms and the smell of cigarette smoke. She confided that she had been to this psych ward multiple times. When I asked about the scars, she explained that her life had caused her so much pain that she coped by cutting herself with a knife and burning herself with the cigarettes she smoked. I didn't ask for further details, and she didn't offer any.

Although I had only just arrived, I asked how anyone got out of here, and she started cackling. Her eyes were tired when she finally stopped; and then she told me that this wasn't a place where you could simply leave when you wanted to, or where anyone could check you out of. The doctors and the doctors alone determined how long you would stay, so you had better be on your best behavior.

This news chilled me, but I swiftly transformed my fear into determination. Not having control over anything was nothing new to me. I would find a way to satisfy the doctors' requirements when I was scheduled to meet them the next day.

A bell rang and my roommate stood up abruptly, noting that there were smoke breaks for patients who smoked a couple times a day. It was going to be the only way I'd see the sun anytime soon, and she advised that I should lie about being a smoker.

I was still easily exhausted and wanted badly to lie down, so I mumbled that I'd stay in. Although she noticed my weariness, she insisted on me coming along. If I refused her idea now, the nurses would not let me go on any future cigarette breaks. Either I needed to lie to them that I was a smoker, or I was going to say goodbye to this opportunity entirely.

I hesitated for a moment, then the memory of Yi's smoke saturated room and his hand ripping at my hair and body hit me. I quietly repeated my refusal, and she left with the nurses and the other smokers.

I slept.

***

I MET WITH THE MENTAL HEALTH DOCTOR the next day. He looked kind at first, and asked that I take a seat as the nurse closed the door behind me. He asked how I was doing, and talked about the rules of the ward, and wrote notes on a sheet of paper in front of him.

He asked me to explain why I had taken the painkillers, and I tried to do it in such a way that they would let me out. My mind scrambled for a good way to give him enough information, but not too much. I didn't want to delve too deeply in my recent past. Not with this guy, anyway.

I asked him what the shortest stay at the psych ward was, and he replied that three days was the absolute minimum stay. Feeling bold, I asked what led him to determine if three days was enough time or not. He paused, lay his pen-bearing hand flat on the paper, and looked me straight in the eye, "Just don't cry. Don't cry for three days. Eat normally, sleep normally, interact with the staff and other patients normally".

He offered to prescribe some pills or sedatives that might help me, but I was barely listening and tried to act calm and polite in my refusal.

Three days of imprisonment and constant observation seemed to be an eternity in this place. I stumbled away from his office after our "therapy" session, feeling cold and sick. I felt my tear ducts well up with despair. I blinked furiously. I had to get out of here.

So, I hung out in the "social" room where patients could congregate under the watchful eyes of the burly-armed nurses. I pulled battered puzzles off the shelves and did crossword puzzles to demonstrate I was healthy enough for these games. I chatted idly on safe topics with nurses and patients, and learned to bite my arm at night to stop from making any sobbing sounds and to hide in the bathroom during a panic attack.

***

THE SECOND NIGHT, there was a big scuffle in the hallway that woke everyone. One of the male patients had received the same news as I'd had; that you could not check out once you were checked in, and only the doctor determined the length of your stay. I guess the hallway wasn't a big enough world for him.

I jolted awake the first time he hurled himself at the fire exit door. There was a loud bang each time his shoulder collided with the metal handle, vibrating against the frame from the force of his rage and desperation. The male nurses strode quickly and purposefully down the hallway towards him, shouting at all the patients to stay in their rooms.

I watched wide-eyed from the small window in the door as they strode by. My room was dark, since it was after hours, but the hallways had been brightly lit due to all the activity. I could not see that far down the hall, but I could hear.

I heard the male patient shout and grunt with effort as he slammed again and again into the door. I heard the nurses tackle him to the floor, heard them punch and kick him into submission, heard him swear at the nurses in pain and anger, heard them drag him to his room.

He was my neighbor, and through the wall, I heard the nurses ask for a tranquilizer to put him to sleep.

***

MY THIRD DAY AT THE FACILITY was a Sunday, visitor day. The nurses asked us all to come up to their counter one by one and everyone was handed pills. I asked my roommate what was going on, and she whispered excitedly that today was the "fun" day. Everyone would be doped up and high, so that when the visitors came, everyone would be happy and pleasant. She advised that I obediently take the pills even though the doctor had explained to me that I had a choice to take pills or to not take pills.

I had declined at that time, because he had also explained that most of the pills required an observation period of one week, and I had no interest in staying a day longer than I had to. But now I was trapped; how would I avoid taking the pills that everyone was taking without appearing rebellious and unfit for discharge?

My roommate was called up, given her pills which she quickly downed with a gulp of water, and opened her mouth wide so that the nurse could see she had swallowed. I was next.

I tried to calm my breathing and appear normal as I smiled and insisted that I was in a relatively good mood today and wondered if I could skip the pills. The nurse hesitated for a moment, but perhaps he remembered that I had been "good" so far; eating my meals dutifully, drinking water when told, etc. We had even chatted normally before. He shrugged and let me go.

Knowing there were nurses and cameras, I interacted as normally as I could with a couple friends who had come to visit. It was much harder to convince them that everything was fine and to steer all conversation away from how the mental care facility was treating me and how I was doing. I anxiously asked them about classes and other friends, and peppered them with safe topics of conversation.

Eventually, it was time for them to go. I smiled as I hugged them, smiled as we said goodbye, smiled as I watched them leave out the door that I could not leave through just yet...

I could feel the nurses watching. I turned to see a nurse staring at me, and let my gaze politely drop when he reached for his pocket pen and jotted notes down on his clipboard.

I sat back down at the table in the social room and returned to a book of crossword puzzles I had been using. I made sure to stay another good thirty minutes, even though I knew I had no other visitors coming. Then, I got up, excused myself, and returned to my room with the crossword puzzle book in my hand to give the impression I was going to keep doing crosswords in my room.

We were not allowed to close the door during active hours, so I merely sat at the desk in my small room and opened the book to a new puzzle and stared blankly at it while I tried to empty my mind and stop tears from forming. I had so many emotions from seeing my friends and being reminded of the outside world and of the freedom I did not have. So, I wrestled with myself for a long while, eventually narrowing my focus again to one thing, being "good", being "normal".

The next day came. My 3rd day. When I met with the doctor, he read the notes about me and decided to let me go. I meekly shuffled out the doors with two of the buff male nurses escorting me. As I heard the metal doors close, I promised myself I would never go back there.

I would either not try to kill myself again, or I would not fail.

37

The school needed to figure out what to do with me. At this point, I was a potential risk.

The university didn't want to risk me—a student—killing myself on campus. It would look bad in the press.

I was hurried in to a meeting with the Dean of Students. He explained that I would not be expelled if I signed some documents promising I wouldn't sue the school. Also, I was going to be put on medical leave immediately. I was required to do a semester worth of weekly counselling, and the counselor would need to send a letter of support for me to return to school in order for me to return to Vanderbilt.

I swallowed hard and quietly confided in him that the chances of me being suicidal and depressed living at home was much higher than if I were allowed to stay at the university. I promised that I would be "good". I begged him to let me stay.

He was unmoved and stared at me flatly, waiting for me to sign the letter. I was eighteen and legally able to sign documents. I didn't have time to read the thick stack of paper—not that I would have comprehended what I was reading. I couldn't believe what he was telling me. But between being expelled and having a chance at going back to school, the choice seemed clear. I signed the paper.

He may have forgotten to mention that when I got back to the dorm, the dorm manager would be waiting to explain that, under the Code of Student Conduct, I was deemed a "disturber of the peace" since I had been crying so much to people about my rape and depression. They declared that it was bothering other students too much and therefore, they were within their rights to kick me out of all the dorms.

I wasn't permitted to live on campus, effective immediately. I wouldn't be permitted to stay the night, but they'd give me a week to visit during the day to move out my stuff. I was in shock, but I didn't have time to fully process my surprise or the feeling of being wronged. I had to be out quickly, and packed everything up in a daze.

* * *

MOM AND DAD FLEW me home. I felt worse than ever. I was returning to the one place from which I had tried to escape.

They made it very clear that I was the shame of the family. They claimed that all the other people in the same graduating class of my high school were doing fantastically and attended amazing schools; and yet here I was, back at home when I should be getting ahead in life, not behind. I should be embarrassed and ashamed. Besides, I wasn't even in a top ten school, only top twenty, and I hadn't even lasted there. I was weak, I was bad, I was worthless. I was a waste of time, money, space.

They asked aloud what the point had been in investing so much energy in raising me. Mom even stated that she should have aborted me like she originally wanted to. Their words cut deep into me, but I succeeded in keeping my emotions from view while I nodded along with their statements.

Mom and Dad invited an army of tutors to fill my days. I rarely went out, dutifully taking all the classes. I took a deep breath, since this was going to be the longest I'd maintained this grueling schedule of tutors.

In the past, I was only put on this packed schedule for the duration of winter or summer vacation, not an entire semester plus summer time. Additionally, I'd have to convince the counselor that I was stable and healthy enough to return to college.

I met with a mental health counselor every week. She was a middle-aged white lady with a kind face. We would talk about the week, and I did my best to talk carefully so as to ensure that she would support my return to campus. Getting out from under Mom and Dad's roof was my top priority.

I fed the counselor chunks of sob stories so that she would feel as though we were actually working through issues. I made sure I cried sometimes, but also wanted to make sure that it wasn't so often that the counselor might think I was not ready for college. She was a nice lady, and I wished we could have actually worked on my issues, but I could not trust her fully. I needed her to write a clean report. I needed to get out of here.

I needed more support than one mock-therapist, though. I don't think I could have made it through those months if it weren't for Kathy. We lived just a few blocks away from one another. She was finishing her senior year at the same high school I had graduated from. I had known her from before, and when I returned home, we reconnected. Kathy and I clung to each other. I didn't know her story or her sorrows, but we met up somehow and became inseparable.

Kathy was the one I actually opened up to completely, diluting a lot of the emotional poison that had built up in me. Mom and Dad felt it was ok for me to hang out with her, as long as it didn't distract me from my classes. I made sure to work hard in my lessons and they allowed me this one friend.

We'd sleep at each other's houses. Oftentimes, Kathy stayed over because both her parents worked and let her be a "free spirit"- they basically neglected her.

Kathy was fascinated with all the random skills I'd picked up from all those tutors over the years, such as painting, singing, dancing, and I loved this rare opportunity to show someone what I had learned and to feel appreciated. I felt happiness with her, and we developed a deep friendship.

38

Kathy and I spent almost every day together. I would meet her after her school day or after she'd done her homework and I'd finished my lessons. I had some form of art class most days, so she'd eagerly come over to see the progress that I had made.

One time, I drew and shaded in old children's toys I had found in the basement, including a medium-sized figure of Mario. She really liked that one. Another time, I painted blue birds and she liked the feathers. Occasionally, she'd come over on days when I had classes and she'd hang out during the lesson.

Occasionally, we would go down to the small plaza of stores and restaurants that was really the only hangout location in the suburban area where we lived. Usually, Kathy would use her electric scooter to avoid the exercise. I typically opted to rollerblade while she rode alongside me. Sometimes, I would hold onto the back of her scooter while she pulled me along on my rollerblades.

Sometimes, with deep reluctance, I would sit behind her on the scooter. I disliked sitting on the back of the scooter since my legs were too long for the small scooter, and if I didn't pull my legs up the whole ride, my feet would drag. The passenger foot pedals were too tiny to be of any use to me, so I would have to use my muscles the whole trip, which was very uncomfortable. On top of that, I was also unfamiliar with riding electric scooters and would feel anxiety despite Kathy being a practiced and confident driver. She always teased me about my discomfort. We never fell, but all the same, I'd yelp when Kathy playfully swerved to get a reaction from me.

Kathy could detect while we were riding alongside one another or if I was rollerblading alongside her when I was in deep thought. She wistfully expressed it felt like I'd gone away from her even though we were hardly more than arm's length apart. I explained that I needed to think of something other than the blistering heat of Beijing summer and my muscles protesting the exercise in order to maintain the speed needed to keep up with her electric scooter.

I didn't like to rest or take a break during our short trip to the plaza, but I had not exercised in a long time when we first began making these trips. My body was still recovering from my not-so-distant hospital visit, but I was stubborn and determined to make it to the plaza without stopping each time, and so we did.

The total distance to the plaza was a little over a forty-five-minute walk. Humid summers made hot—over ninety-degree Fahrenheit—weather extra challenging as I pushed myself to reach the plaza sooner. Since the trip was physically challenging for me, I usually wouldn't speak, especially if I was rollerblading. I could not stand the sound of panting, because it triggered me to think about rape, so I'd control my breathing during the trip. Kathy would join me in silence if she didn't have any stories from the day to share with me.

At the plaza, Kathy and I would sometimes buy candy or ice cream from the store, but my favorite place was the bakery. There was one small bakery there that baked wonderful bread and I loved the smell of it the moment you opened the door. Kathy's Mom often bought German sourdough there and I would beg for it anytime we were at Kathy's house. It reached a point at which Kathy would confidently say she understood just from the look on my face when I was thinking about the bread. She'd chuckle exasperatedly and we'd go to the kitchen so we could each get a slice.

There wasn't much to see at the little plaza, but it was somewhere away from our homes and we would drift around the same restaurants and shops often, despite there being nothing new.

39

My brother had a hip-hop/breakdance teacher as a tutor. Mom invited him to start giving my brother and I lessons. He taught us in English, since he was actually from America.

Over the months, I got to know him and we became friends. He was a fun, cool guy and I found myself opening up to him about my recent past. He felt safe and I trusted him.

He had a long-term girlfriend who was a dancer that I greatly admired. Plus, he was close friends with my brother, hanging out with him often after classes and on weekends. A compassionate person, he was horrified by what I had been through.

Over the months, he also earned the trust of Mom and Dad. They liked that my brother hung out with him, hoping that the teacher could keep an eye on their wild son and help him stay out of serious trouble. Occasionally, he hosted parties at his apartment, and my brother was allowed to go. One time when he invited me, I asked Mom and Dad for permission.

To my surprise, Mom and Dad let me go to this house party. My brother and other students and friends liked to meet up at his apartment and there would be drinking and games. I had not yet been to any of these parties. Mom and Dad felt it was safe enough for me to go what with my brother already having been several times.

So, my brother and I went to the party together. I had never gone to a house party before. Especially after having seen what binge drinking had done to my brother thus far, I wasn't particularly one for drinking. But it was nice to be allowed out this one night.

I didn't want to get tipsy, so I sipped lightly on my drinks and did not participate in the drinking games. Everyone became progressively more drunk as the drinking games went by. Although I had laughed along as the others became silly in their drunkenness, my laughter swiftly stopped when it was clear that everyone had a little bit too much. Nearly all the drinking game players—including my brother—were throwing up from consuming too much alcohol. I rushed around to take care of and clean up after everyone.

By the early hours of the morning, I was thoroughly exhausted from cleaning everyone's vomit, including my brother's. He was passed out on the couch, unable to be awakened by my efforts, and everyone started tottering towards beds and couches.

I didn't know if I should stay or go. I could have left my brother and called a cab I guess, although I don't recall if I had any cash on me. Probably not. It was far too late in the night to call Mom and Dad to pick me up. I didn't even have a key to the house, so I would have had to wake them or take my brother's garage key.

I struggled to decide what to do. While I hesitated, the dance teacher told me that all that was left was his room, but it had a massive king size bed and we could sleep far apart. "It'll be fine," he said, "trust me."

Exhaustion helped make my decision. I hadn't stayed up this late in a long time, and I was extremely tired. Besides, my brother was still sleeping there on the couch. I lay down gingerly on my side of the king bed—as far away as I could from the dance teacher—and closed my eyes. I began to drift off to sleep because I was comfortable with the teacher. I was safe. I closed my eyes.

The next moment, he was snuggling up to me, pressing against me; his dick was hard and his hands explored my body. I almost had time to scream before I felt my conscious control slip away, my triggers activated. I would be his sex toy now, doing all the things my first boyfriend conditioned me to do, unable to stop myself, unable to face what was happening. I think in therapist speak it's called "severe dissociation". I went away and let my triggered version of myself take over for the duration of this unwanted act.

And when I came back to myself later, I cried. I cried for the shame, cried for the helplessness, cried for this recurring event. I cried over the betrayal, cried over my foolishness for thinking that—since he was in a committed relationship with a more attractive, flexible, loving partner and I was just an awkward, depressed, beginner level student barely nineteen years old now—I would be safe.

My brother is still friends with him. I tried telling my own blood sibling what had happened, and he shook his head incredulously that I was making it up or just regretting the sex and mislabeling it. He called me a slut.

I didn't bother trying to speak to Mom and Dad about it; I already knew what they would have said. They would have said I deserved it; because I agreed to sleep on the same mattress, I agreed to the act. Besides, to them I was still that "whore", "sex crazy bitch", "waste of money/life/time/effort" daughter who had dated my first boyfriend and had been kicked out of my not-even-that-great school.

* * *

I BLAMED MYSELF FOR what had happened. I felt ashamed. Despite all that I had experienced under the hands of Yi and Luke, here I was in the same situation again. I had trusted again, been naive about the thoughts a man had about me, and failed to understand their attraction to me or to the act of sex or rape.

I questioned my experience. I felt that he should have known I didn't want this and that this was wrong. He was in a relationship. I had thought that would matter. She was prettier, in the same line of business as him, a dancer, and therefore more flexible and just better in every single way.

I had not worn anything pretty or suggestive. I had worn no makeup. I had not done anything to flirt with him or encourage this kind of behavior. I had never been nor was I currently interested in him romantically or sexually.

So, why? Why? Why?

Nothing made sense. He apologized to me, insisted he felt bad and should have known better. Knowing I had nowhere to really let my emotions out and cry, he let me come over and I felt I had nothing left to lose and nowhere to turn, so I did. I wanted to turn back time to where none of this had happened.

I still trusted him enough that I felt he wouldn't do it again. And this time he didn't break that trust. I told him honestly how it made me feel, and he tried to apologize. We visited a few more times like this, and although our relationship could never be repaired, his willingness to listen to my pain and willingness to apologize made me feel a little better.

I did not hate him, but I could not be friends with him anymore. I lied and told Mom and Dad I didn't like hip hop and breakdancing after all, and convinced them that I was also concerned about becoming stronger and more muscular. They agreed and switched this lesson to yoga with another teacher instead.

I made sure not to share any of these events with my mock counselor. I did not want to jeopardize my return to Vanderbilt.

I soldiered on.

40

One day, I decided that if I just kept assuming my parents would not support me, then I would never be giving them a chance.

I was not sure how to broach the subject of what I had experienced in college, and was aware of how sensitive they still were on the subject of Yi. I was also very nervous about talking to them—unsure of what their response would be. Mom was relatively more approachable, so I felt that it was safer to test the waters by speaking to her on this topic.

After thinking back and forth about how to initiate the conversation, I hatched a lame plan of talking to Mom in hypotheticals. When I had a chance to have a one-on-one conversation, I gathered my courage to ask her, "What do you think about rape in terms of Chinese culture? How is it handled in Chinese culture?" I shared with her the statistic that one in four women in college experienced some form of sexual harassment, assault, or rape.

Mom seemed surprised by this line of questioning, but not suspicious. She observed aloud that it was unfortunate what had happened to the victims, but in her understanding of Chinese culture, it was a mistake to report.

I was stunned by this statement and asked for her to elaborate. She told me simply that it was very shameful to be raped, and that it would be shameful to not just the victim, but to the victim's family as well.

They would all feel "窝囊" (wo nang) — or deeply humiliated, helpless, and powerless. It would be pointless to make others feel bad due to one person's misfortune.

She advised it was best to just hide the shame and speak to no one about the rape, including authorities. She believed that it hurt the victim's marriage prospects if word got out and may even cause them to lose friends because of how disgusting that experience was.

I doggedly continued the topic, despite the torrent of emotions I was experiencing. Recklessly, I put myself into the next question, barely veiling my line of questioning.

"Mom, what if I was raped in college and I wanted to report it?"

There were no tears, no antics. She stopped for a moment and raised an eyebrow. I could tell she didn't believe that her daughter could experience such a thing. In her mind, it was impossible that such a tragedy could befall me or the family. Despite how obvious my questioning was, she still believed it was just hypothetical.

She frowned in concentration as she imagined what she would do and what I should do in this make-believe situation. Then she began talking about the implications of reporting the rape and how that could affect Dad and the family. Since Dad was a high-ranking executive that occasionally appeared in the press, I too, might even appear in a news story and that would be mortifying for everyone; did I really want to do that to Dad?

She rattled on about how, if police were involved, that could lead to court fees and all that would just be so expensive and probably wouldn't even lead to anything significant in terms of punishment for the rapist.

I nodded numbly and let the subject drop. I didn't talk to her about this topic again.

41

Keeping everything bottled up began affecting me more and more. I felt the need to reach out and talk to someone. I eventually ended up sharing everything with Kathy; I told her all the things that had happened to me. I talked to her as I had talked with the dance teacher.

Confiding in a girlfriend seemed to be a healthy and good choice. She was safe. She couldn't possible desire me, right? She would not betray me as the dance teacher did, would she?

Kathy didn't. She was the best listening ear and shoulder for support I could have had. "Friends are amazing", I thought to myself, "I wish I could have this forever". For the first time I felt like I wasn't alone.

* * *

PERHAPS KATHY WAS TOO YOUNG and fragile for the realities of the world I had experienced. I had not considered the impact of learning about my story and how it would affect her. She put on a good front and even convinced me for several weeks that everything was fine.

Then one day, I caught her wincing and clutching her arm. I insisted on seeing what was hurting her. I expected to see a bruise from something random.

Kathy did not try hard to hide her wound from me. She had been cutting herself on her arm, close to the inside of her elbow so that her parents wouldn't see. She broke down and confessed that she hadn't been able to cope with the information I'd told her. She felt so awful and helpless that she had turned to self-harm to alleviate the pain.

I immediately felt responsible. I was horrified. Perhaps Mom was right about it being wrong to share my story with others. Perhaps the university was right and I was a "disturber of the peace", a threat to others. With great sadness, I felt the need to end our friendship to stop my life from hurting her.

But first, I had to make sure she stopped cutting herself. I did not turn to her family for help, since my family had never been there for me. I also did not believe in reaching out to counselors or mental care services, since those had not been good for me, either. I did the only thing I could think of.

I listened. I hugged her over nights where she cried and told me of the pain of listening to my stories. I encouraged her to talk about anything and everything.

She poured out all her emotions to me. She cried about her fear, her sadness, feeling my pain through my stories, her helplessness at really not being able to do anything about it. I apologized and apologized. I hid my feelings from her. I felt responsible for raping her mind. I was a monster.

After that, I resolved to not talk about my abuse experiences again—at least not in so much detail. Kathy gradually felt better and the cutting stopped. I made sure to be as supportive as I could and to have as much fun and happiness with her as possible towards the tail end of that summer. I tried to keep her smiling and laughing. I knew I was going to say goodbye.

Summer ended, and Kathy went to college. In the beginning, we were still having frequent video and phone calls. I couldn't let go. Then, on one call, she mentioned in passing that there was a party going on but she'd rather talk with me.

It was a sweet thing to say, but I was afraid that I was again negatively influencing her life. I felt she should be out there doing fun college things, living life, instead of being held back or affected by me. I was ruining her college experience.

That hardened my resolve. I cut ties with her. I told her she needed to make friends with other people, instead of relying on me. I refused to answer her calls. I was very cold. This made her angry and sad. She didn't understand my sudden rejection, but when she failed to revive our usual relationship, she eventually let go. As I'd hoped, she left me and went to live her own college life.

Through social media, I could see that it seemed to have worked. I confess I stalked her online, hoping she was happy and making friends. After a few months, she seemed to have found a core group of friends, and I was relieved. I hoped they could make her smile and laugh. I hoped she lived her life to the fullest. I felt I'd done the right thing. Satisfied that she seemed happy and safe, I stopped following her posts.

Years later, I attempted to communicate with her a couple times to apologize and try to reconnect, but I found that she still strongly resented me. I couldn't blame her when she blocked and deleted me. I was sad, but also glad that she had the strength to block and delete people who she felt were a negative impact on her life.

42

I felt very alone, but just as before, I thought that perhaps flying away and going to college would solve my problems. At least, leaving home meant that I would not have to deal with Mom and Dad on a daily basis. I prayed my designated counselor would write to the college to support my return. And she did.

The university received the letter from my counselor and they, in turn, sent me a letter that stated I was no longer on mandatory medical leave. The dorms reluctantly opened their doors to me again and I breathed a sigh of relief.

As part of the agreement for me to return to university, I was to have periodic visits with the Dean of Students as well as a counselor to ensure that I was not going to be a danger to myself or others.

I told the school that the pressure of being forced to take a major I didn't want had caused me to fall apart. They seemed to swallow the story, and it wasn't all a lie after all; it merely didn't cover everything. I changed my major status to "Undecided". So now what was I going to do?

I decided the only way to know for sure what I would excel in and enjoy, would be to take classes in all the departments the university offered. I had already tried my hand at engineering, and decided to try everything from criminology to music writing. I packed as many classes as I could into my schedule. I would find myself taking math, history, short story writing, and coding some semesters. I was everywhere.

As a result, my classes were so scattered all over campus that the break between classes would not be sufficient for me to make it there on time if I were to walk. I did not want to get a bike for fear that someone would steal the seat or the wheels, as often happened. The campus was littered with skeletons of bikes still locked to the bike rack, but missing various parts. Instead, I bought a pair of rollerblades, and that was how I commuted to all my classes.

I'd keep my rollerblades on the whole class, and I'd glide to the front of the room if the teacher called me to come up and get my papers. Luckily, this amused the students and teachers alike. They never banned me from rollerblading in class and I developed a small reputation. They called me "Roller Girl".

43

Alongside classes, I also regularly saw the newly assigned mental health professional each week. Since this counselor would not have power or influence over my continuation of school, I opened up to her a lot more. Over months and months of therapy, we tried several different approaches to help me work through my trauma. Our goal was to reduce the number of panic attacks and nightmares I had in a week so that I could attend all classes and hopefully live normally.

One of the more bizarre methods for me was hypnosis or meditation. She would alternate tapping at my left and right palm with a pen while asking me to focus on my memories of the past. The idea was to start with the slightly less horrifying ones and work our way towards the most painful ones. However, we found that hypnosis did not work on me. I just sat there awkwardly while she tapped and tapped.

Another method was self-help style methods. She encouraged me to develop the habit of standing in certain poses in front of a mirror called "power poses" while repeating positive statements about myself. These were supposed to help me with the negativity that Mom and Dad had instilled in me throughout my life. This felt awkward, too, and I often lied that I had done it all week when in reality, I had barely given it a single, half-hearted try. I felt very silly even imagining myself standing there vocalizing these "empowering" messages. It felt dumb. My voice sounded weak and unconvincing, and eventually, I gave up entirely on this approach.

The most productive item was working through some of my triggers. She had me list every single trigger I could think of. It was an extremely long list that we tackled one by one. Occasionally, this meant forcing me into a panic attack during a session so she could observe and help me through it. Some of my triggers reduced in intensity as a result, but not all.

The therapist also had me journal or just try remembering as much as I possibly could and share my memories with her. This was a terrible experience, and at first, it felt as though we were going backwards, given that my panic attacks exploded in frequency.

My attendance and grades suffered, my attention span dropped, and everything became worse. Consciously choosing to relive these traumatic memories was overwhelmingly painful. It was an extremely tough time.

Little by little, I developed a better grip on consciously thinking about each memory so that I was not paralyzed every time I remembered anything. I was careful not to talk to anyone about my struggles, except with this counselor. I was unsure of how other students would handle anything I shared with them and didn't want to get in trouble again. I didn't talk about my past with any of my peers. My friendships with others felt shallow and unfulfilling.

Somehow, I managed to juggle therapy sessions and academics. I was determined to not give the university any reason to kick me out. I was very careful with my public behavior and talks with any staff members. Remembering what I had learned at the ward about portraying "healthy" behavior, I pushed myself to perform.

I joined various student clubs partly to demonstrate that everything was fine and partly out of curiosity. I even co-founded a club. This new club actually became a robust student club dedicated to Chinese learning and culture sharing that exists to this day. I'm proud to have been involved in the birth of a club that has brought hundreds of people together and will hopefully continue to do so.

I continued to explore various majors and take a wide variety of classes. Although my grades were not always up to my parents' standards, and most everything was unfamiliar to me, I did as best I could and ended up with Dean's List a few times (Dean's List Honors are given to students who complete a minimum of 12 graded credits in a semester with a GPA of at least 3.500). Although this was worthless to my parents since it wasn't a 4.0 and Vanderbilt would never be Harvard or Stanford to them, I was quietly happy about my achievement.

Eventually, academically, I found a place in which I belonged. I'd never thought I'd end up where I did.

I found my calling in a random art class. After creating a few paintings in class, I suddenly felt more alive. I loved mixing the colors, sitting in the solace of the studio, painting what I pleased. I'd stay late into the night, when the art building would be empty, save for one or two other students.

I spent many hours in the studio, mostly because I had to practice a lot. Everyone else who was an art major had been dedicated to art since elementary or middle school. Yet, here I was, with absolutely no background in the arts, trying to make it as an art major. I hadn't even been a doodler in grade school. My technique and foundational skills were nonexistent.

I painted and drew many drills and exercises to overcome my lack of skill and experience. Over time, my drawings improved; my paintings drew compliments, and I was happy.

44

I made a new group of friends, whom I met as I randomly rolled into the dorm building after class one day. They were playing Dance Revolution (DDR) in the common room. I had played the game a couple years before, and had a lot of fun. They noticed my interest, and beckoned me to join them.

I took off my roller blades to sit and watch. They warmly offered me a turn and we laughed and played until we were all breathless. They knew I was the Roller Girl, and we chatted for a time, discovering that our rooms were not far apart. Although I wasn't very good, we all had fun and they invited me to come again next week.

We started eating together at the cafeteria, and playing DDR each Friday. The next year when it came time to change dorms, I roomed with them and we hung out every day.

Spring break came and we decided to take a road trip to one of the girls' mom's timeshare next to Disney World. I hadn't been to Disney for several years, and couldn't wait to go. I was extra excited because my birthday was going to coincide with us being there, and I'd get a free day to go to one of the parks, wearing a "It's My Birthday" pin. I was over the moon!

It rained on the morning of my birthday. I woke up early so that I could be at the gates the moment the park opened to visitors. I shook my roommate awake and we pulled on clothes, her a little slower than me.

The other girls wanted to sleep in or save their money, and I was disappointed since they had all promised to spend my birthday with me at the park. I stomped out the door, determined to have fun despite the rain and not having all my friends with me. I was going to the park alone, if I had to.

My roommate, Jada, staunchly stated she would still come with me—rain or no rain. I beamed. Arm in arm we went to the park. The sky started clearing up by mid-morning and the sun came out, as if the rainy-day morning had never happened. It was a glorious day with rainbows and sunshine.

The Disney characters greeted me and wished me hundreds of "happy birthdays". I ran around grabbing all the hugs I could get from Disney characters, Jada in tow. We had so much fun! I was so glad she was there to keep me company. My heart felt full.

* * *

ONE OF THE THINGS this group did regularly, was gift wrap someone's door when it was their birthday. We would plan a time where enough of us weren't in class, but our "victim" was. We'd have a lookout in the hallway, in case she came back early. The lookout also acted as taskmaster in case we were giggling more than getting the job done.

Two people would wrap the door quickly, cutting a neat hole for the door handle and lock so that the individual could leave their door decorated for several days with ease of entry and exit. We'd find colorful and shiny gift-wrapping paper and cover the entire door. If someone's birthday was on a break, we'd wrap their door before or after, but this tradition was always followed.

As the newest addition to the group, and as timing would have it, I'd be the last door to wrap of this semester. There had been no secretive looks and random giggles between the other girls, so I knew that it hadn't been planned before spring break; but I figured surely, after our Disney spring break, they would wrap my door.

I went about my days as usual and my door remained unwrapped. It took a while, but I stopped anticipating coming back from class to see a beautifully gift-wrapped door. I continued hanging out with the girls, but I compartmentalized them as surface friends after that, save for Jada. I felt rejected in a way. I felt I would never be one of them, but I could still have fun with them for the time being. So, I did.

45

I developed interest in a smiley giant named Steve. He had a great belly laugh, was very playful, worked out often, and was in ROTC. I still had fears from my past, and I thought perhaps his muscles could protect me from the ghosts that haunted me. I felt happy and safe with him. He found me attractive and we got close, started dating, kissing, and sleeping together. As I relaxed, I started confiding in him about my past.

But this was a mistake. Steve, like Kathy, couldn't handle the information. I had not gone into the same level of detail as before, but it appeared that what I did tell him was still too much information. Steve developed nightmares, moodiness, and depression. He would rage at the abusers in my past, threatening to kill them if he had the chance, as he squeezed me tightly in his arms.

One day, weary from nights of not sleeping well due to me waking him up from my panic attacks, he broke down and told me he wasn't strong enough to support me and comfort me any longer. There was too much pain in my stories. He said his grades were slipping, he had stopped liking me in "that way", and he had to let me go. I understood and I didn't want to hurt him. So, we broke up.

He started dating another girl a few days after our breakup and recovered much of his cheerful nature. I guess she had less dark of a past, and she was definitely better for him.

I was happy for him, but I also felt a faint ache in my heart that I couldn't put words to. I felt confused when he boasted loudly one day about how many points he had earned from sleeping with so many girls.

We were in a large room of mutual friends. Some people looked awkwardly at me and there was a brief hush around the room, since I was one of the "points". I looked away.

46

Losing Steve as part of my emotional support when I had just begun to open up again, was devastating. I became increasingly anxious about losing support. I realized also that having my current counselor wouldn't last forever. Once I completed college and presumably moved away, I would no longer be able to see her. I felt I needed to find strength on my own as soon as possible.

I began attending self-help seminars, reading related books, and doing mental exercises on my own. My biggest fear of all was physical contact, especially with men other than the rare few that I deemed safe. The mere thought of it was enough to make me shiver uncontrollably. I needed to find a way to overcome this.

I decided to use a brute force method to confront this fear. I threw myself into a ballroom dancing class. This forced me to follow the lead of a male, usually someone I did not know, and dance gracefully. I focused intensely on the music and tried not to recoil at the initial contact of his hands.

The first classes were hard, I would maintain my composure as I left the dance studio, then run to the car. Slamming the door shut, I'd have a mini panic attack as quietly as I could. I would clutch my arms hard to my sides, pressing hard into my skin so that the pain would help distract from the panic that threatened to envelop me.

I continued attending the classes, learning the basic steps for waltz, tango, salsa, cha cha, and others. I paired up with strangers in class and during their weekend social dances. I tried to dance lightly and gracefully, learning to take back control of my body and mind.

Physical contact became easier, and in time, I even began to be decent at dance. Although I could not stop my skin from becoming chilled at the touch of a stranger's hand, I learned through sheer determination not to be as distressed by physical contact. I learned to enjoy dance, even winning an Amateur Tangoist award in a local dance competition.

47

I became a bit of a loner. My time was divided between classes, dance, practicing in the art studio, and playing video games.

I developed an aptitude for a first-person shooting game. My favorite was called "Left for Dead 2", a zombie shooting game where a team of four survivors attempted to get from point A to point B with at least one person making it out alive. I became the person at the head of the pack who set the pace, speeding swiftly through and plowing a path through zombie-filled malls and parks with my trusty shotgun and various weapons.

My favorite weapon was the katana. With it, I'd carve a bloody trail through enemy zombies that tried to kill us. My friends would follow me with mid-range or long-range weapons to take out any threats that I missed or could not reach.

There weren't—and still aren't—that many girl gamers in shooting games, and I often received plenty of extra anger from bitter, defeated opponents who couldn't believe they had been defeated by a *girl*. It made me smile.

This time of self-imposed isolation gave me a lot of time for self-discovery. Who was I?

I resolved to try out other lifestyles, similar to how I had been trying classes from all different departments to find my calling.

I spent one semester as a social butterfly, attending all the parties, dressing up cute, using makeup (but not all of the time), being flirty and fun, and always issuing invites to dine out or go on adventures together. I was surprised to learn that I had the ability to be the life of the party, if I chose to be that. It appeared that I had enough charisma to pull people together and enough sensitivity to make sure everyone had a good time. However, I didn't enjoy being so social, so I moved on to try other things.

Although I had co-founded a club, I had left that club for others. Beyond getting it started, I had not been a leader there. On a whim, I joined the juggling club. Over the semesters I became more involved with the club, climbed through the ranks, and eventually became president and director. I was president for one year and directed a two-act show that drew in more audience members than any other student-directed shows.

It was during this time that I met and developed a major crush on the previous president of the juggling club, Daniel. Daniel was a natural leader; considerate, mature, and articulate. He had a nice face with blue, boyish eyes, and freckled skin. He had a full beard, which made him look a bit older. His fuzziness made me want to pet him.

We started dating, falling in love. He taught me all he knew about being president of a club, and what he knew of being a successful leader, and brainstormed ideas for juggling choreography with me. I enjoyed our conversations and appreciated his advice about leading. We ate together, slept together, talked to each other about our hopes and dreams. We even ended up meeting each other's parents.

Marriage was a topic that we were not shy to discuss, and he began to think of us as guaranteed to go down that path. I had less confidence.

I had never been interested in marriage before. I wanted to be free to find my path in the world. I remembered how Mom had described marriage to me and how marriage in combination with children had essentially ended her original hopes and dreams. Daniel didn't press me too hard on the subject; we were so young, after all.

We moved in together, learning to accommodate each other's life habits. He was Southern, a gentleman, holding doors open and making sure he was on the road side of the sidewalk, keeping me on the inside. We'd stroll around with my arm curled around his or hand-in-hand.

He appreciated my art, and I supported and encouraged him in his engineering. He hugged me in the nights when I cried over my nightmares and horrors of the past. With him, I felt safe and loved and I did my best for him to feel loved also.

48

College came to an end. We graduated. Neither of us had job prospects at the time.

I took the Meyer's Briggs test, which is meant to indicate potential career choices that match your interests and aptitudes. None of my top ten included a career with art. I was disappointed, and discarded my test results. I was in a limbo state again, not sure what to do with my life. Dad found me an internship, so that seemed better than nothing.

Daniel had less luck. He couldn't find a job anywhere, despite his bachelor's degree in Chemical Engineering. I didn't know how to help. Dad said he would cosign and help pay for a nice apartment if he chose where we lived, and we agreed. I began working at the internship.

As the months went on, Daniel's frustration with not being able to assist in paying bills, receiving rejections or no answers to his job applications, started to wear on him. He had big dreams, goals, and ambitions. He wanted to be able to buy nice things, pay the bills, or at least share them so that we no longer relied on my dad and he was nowhere near any of that. He constantly had dark moods, and turned to online games for escape; of course, this did not help him move closer to his goal of getting employed, but it temporarily relieved him of his pain.

Daniel's anger had to go somewhere and it started to manifest itself in our relationship. He'd drive angrily when someone cut him off, swearing violently. Sometimes he'd swerve so sharply, that I feared for our lives.

My distress did not deter him. He started throwing things and couldn't stand it if I was better than him in games. I was so sad watching him spiral out of control, but I did not know how to stop it. I carried more and more responsibilities in the relationship; doing more chores, taking care of both of us, being more supportive—but I also had limits.

I began to tire and became depressed from watching him game rather than apply energy towards his job search. I was also exasperated at his pride. He believed that graduating from Vanderbilt should have landed him a job immediately, and wouldn't tolerate any positions that didn't pay him a certain amount of money. He had rejected what he considered to be "lesser" positions.

I felt that his expectations were unrealistic. I gradually lost my respect for him after months of his tantrums. After the first time he displayed violent behavior and broke his headset, I remembered Yi and how I never wanted to go back to a relationship of violence.

When I told him that I was thinking of leaving, he cried, begged me to stay, and told me he'd work on his anger management issues. Perhaps we had that talk too late. I found myself heartbroken and void of patience. The next time he threw something, I wiped my tears, packed up my things, and left.

I told him that my dad had agreed to pay for one more month of rent and then the lease would be ended.

49

It was in this moment, where I had just lost this person who I had loved deeply, that Dad brought down a crushing blow. Dad reminded me that I was worthless without him and that this internship was because of his connections. He threatened that he could take it away at any moment. Without him, I had no job and seemingly no future.

Dad insisted I should take my packed things and return home to China. I was already struggling with the loneliness of a fresh breakup on top of everything else. I couldn't handle fighting off this negativity alone. I dove into a deep depression.

My gamer friends continued shooting zombies with me as I became more and more reckless in my gameplay. I'd play sloppily and die over and over, unlike before. I began buying small bottles of painkillers, even pouring the bright red pills over the bed, spreading them with my fingers, cupping them in my palms, and remembering college.

At night, I would have nightmares and panic attacks, calling names and repeating futile things to ghosts from my past; phrases that hadn't stopped them before and would not stop them now. I could still feel their rage, their skin, their desire, their lips, their bodies, pinning me down even though they were nowhere near me. I could lock the door, but I couldn't lock them out of my mind except in games—an alternate reality. I gamed most hours of the day, barely taking breaks to take care of myself, and barely sleeping.

I deteriorated far faster than I had healed. I was experiencing panic attacks up to six times a day, and felt completely useless. I believed I was a useless piece of shit, just as Dad had described. I was barely able to focus on anything, barely able to play games, and barely able to hold a conversation. I was weak—physically and mentally.

I voiced a desire to take my own life one day and one of my gamer friends, an older one, told me that I needed help. We didn't even know each other's real names, but he and his wife offered to take me under their wing until Mom and Dad laid off the pressure or I recovered enough to stop having suicidal thoughts.

By this time, I was a skinny little thing, having lost interest in meals. I figured I had nothing left to lose and it might be interesting to meet a gamer friend that I had known so long and trusted. I could always take my life later if I so chose.

They lived in another state, so I checked my bank account, bought the tickets, paid for the shipping of my belongings, and took off.

50

My gamer friend told me his name, Soren, when he picked me up from the airport. He was in his mid-thirties and worked as a manager at an electronics shop. I had lost so much of the progress I had made, that I could barely stand being in the same car with him. It was as if I'd never done therapy at all.

As he drove us back to him and his wife's townhouse, I struggled with keeping a panic attack at bay. Being in the same room was less hard, but still challenging. I struggled not to fall apart.

Soren's wife calmed me down as she me settled into their extra bedroom.

Over the following days and weeks, Soren encouraged me to eat, to sleep. He'd let me hang out in his man cave in the basement. I'd fall asleep on the couch behind him, listening to him talk to the other guys while they shot up zombies. Under his encouragement, I disconnected from the world, told Mom and Dad they'd hear from me in a couple months, turned off my phone, and focused on recovery. And little by little, I began to feel better.

Slowly, by bribing me with my favorite foods, Soren helped me develop enough flesh to cover my ribs, and I felt healthier than I had in a long while.

But something wasn't right, and I learned what that was when Soren's wife went to visit her sister in London. I was alone in the house with Soren, and Soren wanted something from me—something I hadn't anticipated. One time, I was just pulling myself back together from a particularly bad panic attack, when I realized Soren's hands were roaming my body greedily, taking in the curves that had just begun to return.

I was still confused and disoriented from my panic attack. What was happening? Was this part of my panic attack? Was I hallucinating? I looked around me, all of a sudden not sure where I was. For a moment, I thought I could smell Yi's cigarette smoke when I knew there was none.

Soren's hands continued to travel my body and he dragged me closer. I felt myself fall away and disassociate as he reached under my shirt, under my clothes, to feel my cold skin. I closed my eyes and disconnected completely.

I could not understand—could not comprehend—why he, of all people, could betray me like this. Being married, being so much older than me, and me being this bony, starved thing—helpless and ill, not dressing up at all because I felt like and looked like shit— how could he find me desirable?

I still needed help to remember to eat and drink. Most days, I moved between panic attack and dazed resting and then back to panic attack again. On bad days, I could have up to six panic attacks of varying length and severity. And yet, this was happening. This body, my body, is what he chose to grope and fondle and pull towards him on the couch.

Nothing made sense. I felt the weight of my past and the present crushing me.

I was not healed enough to stop his advances. When I dissociated, I had no control over myself. When I was conscious, I felt helpless. I had nowhere to go. I felt that Soren was the only person holding me to this world and if I were to lose his support, I would lose whatever little that I had.

In despair, I let him caress me, let him lick me, kiss me, let him strip me, let him do what he wanted to do to this body—this body that was clearly not mine. Maybe this was just what life had in store for me. Perhaps I would always be someone's thing, someone's toy.

* * *

OVER THE NEXT FEW DAYS every time Soren wanted me, I reactivated the conditioning I'd received from my first boyfriend and disassociated completely from reality. I hated myself. Hated this body. Hated him.

When Soren's wife returned from her trip, we kept her in the dark. I didn't dare tell her the truth. It was this, being homeless, or returning home, which I couldn't contemplate—wouldn't consider.

Soren and his wife had been planning a vacation to Jamaica and they encouraged me to come with them so I wouldn't be alone at the townhouse. I still had enough funds to afford it and I didn't feel strong enough to be alone at a nearby hotel. I figured with Soren's wife around, he would not try anything while we were in Jamaica. So, I went.

While we were there, something unexpected happened. There was a hurricane, and the resort suffered damage. The island lost power for a while. Although the hotel had backup generators, most of the staff working there were missing roofs and missing electricity at home. Reportedly, first day after the storm, eighty percent of the island did not have power. There were palm fronds strewn everywhere and the previously sparkling clear ocean water was choppy and filled with debris.

I felt awful and guilty eating the meals prepared by the restaurant staff who had only storm shelters left to return to. I felt spoiled. I looked at them and thought that they had nothing, and yet here they were, still doing their jobs, still smiling, still giving, still kind.

I tried picking up debris on the pathways to assist hotel staff, but was told I'd just get them in trouble and they had a handle on things. I felt I could accomplish little being only able to help with my bare hands, and they were not allowed to share their tools with me so that I could be of more use. I gave up and wandered awkwardly back to my room.

Seeing the staff and their strength in light of this recent natural disaster gave me a boost of strength. All of them seemed to be functioning and even happy still. I wanted to be strong like them.

* * *

SOREN STARTED SHARING HIS THOUGHTS of leaving his wife with me. He wanted for us to be a couple instead. I asked him to tell his wife the truth about what had transpired. He pushed back and insisted that it wasn't necessary for her to know this hurtful information, especially if he was calling off their marriage. Eventually, he moved out of the townhouse that they had shared for nearly a decade and took me with him to a small studio apartment.

At the end of the day, I wasn't her. I couldn't cook and clean the same way she did, didn't have the same rituals and all the life skills that she had. Soren sank into a deep depression. Sometimes, he raged at me about the changes in his life. He bitterly regretted his decision.

Not knowing any other options, and fearing that Soren's rage would increase and be taken out on me eventually, I reached out to Mom and Dad who offered to pay for me to move out and fly to San Francisco, California. I was relieved but also sad that Soren was suffering. I felt like it was my fault at least somewhat. If I had never come into his life, none of this would have happened.

My parents had their own reasons for sending me to San Francisco. They wanted me there to keep an eye on my brother who would soon start college. They put me at an apartment close by to his college. They ordered me to study for the GMAT, a standardized test for an MBA. If I were enrolled at my brother's school and studying toward an MBA, I could keep an even closer eye on him to make sure he didn't end up in jail or in a hospital. They were afraid there might be a repeat of the drunk driving incident.

I didn't have much of a choice. By this time, I was out of funds and Soren was just about done with me, too. I accepted their offer and boarded the plane. I never talked to or saw Soren again.

51

The apartment my parents picked for me allowed for pets, which was something I had longed for as a child.

After I was settled, I went to a local animal shelter. A staff member at the shelter led me around, introducing me to each pet and told me their names and a little of their background. She took me from stall to stall, and I pet all the animals that accepted me. Of course, I couldn't take them all home, but while I was there, I could at least give them a bit of love and attention.

The last stall we went to had a half-grown black kitten called Monte Carlo. As a black cat he had a tough time finding a forever home. He was so sweet and playful that I couldn't help myself but play a little longer with him than I had with the others. While I teased him with a feather toy, the staff member shared with me a bit more about him.

As luck would have it, another girl had come in and used her birthday money to pay for Monte's adoption fee earlier that day. Her family visited the shelter often and could not take in any more pets, so instead, they sometimes made donations so that pets could be more easily adopted.

I whispered a silent thank you to that young girl, knowing in my heart that I was going to take Monte home. Monte seemed to know too, roaming around my legs and purring outrageously. I signed the papers, bought some basic supplies at the shelter so that the money would go towards taking care of more shelter pets, and took Monte home.

* * *

ALTHOUGH ADORABLE, MONTE WAS by no means easy to get used to. I had never had a pet before and was learning about a lot of things for the first time.

At first, we struggled to find our peace with each other. He wanted to be active at night, and I wanted to sleep. Locking him up with his litter box and water bowl in the bathroom at night wasn't an option. He would meow loudly, paw at the door incessantly, and find ways to be a noisy nuisance. If I let him out of the bathroom, he'd leap at my toes and try to bat at them when I was trying to rest. Sleep was near impossible, but I resolved to find a way to make things work.

We went to war. I was not about to flip my sleep schedule over for this mischievous cat, as much as I liked him. So, we battled. I'd poke at him throughout the day with toys I'd bought him, flicking the feather toy about, tossing around mouse toys filled with catnip, and beaming the laser pointer all around the apartment.

At night, he would scrabble at my feet, trying to catch an undefended toe. Sometimes, he'd walk on top of me or use me as a leaping platform to chase his invisible friends.

Eventually, I won, and he learned to sleep peacefully at night. He would curl up in a tight, round ball at the foot of the bed or next to me. Monte would follow me from room to room, keeping me company. His presence reminded me that he needed to eat and therefore, I needed to eat. He needed water and therefore, I too needed to drink.

I loved him more than I loved myself and he helped restore a little warmth back in my heart. He was incapable of betraying my trust in the way that people had done. He didn't try to use my body, except for petting or warmth, and I relaxed. Memories of Soren faded while I studied my GMAT materials with Monte by my side.

Mom and Dad felt that an MBA would make me more employable and help me earn a better salary. Dad even briefly sent Mom to San Francisco to make sure I was studying.

The maximum score for the test was 800, and most of the top business schools were looking for scores of at least over 700. The first score I received was only 640 and I got an earful, but a few months later, I scored 720 and that was good enough to please Dad. I applied and was accepted to the MBA program for the school that my brother was going to for his undergrad studies. I breathed a sigh of relief for being able to do what Mom and Dad asked and being a student again – a role I was familiar and comfortable with.

52

While I waited for my first semester at the MBA program to start, Dad found me an internship again, and I went meekly. The small amount of belief I had started to build in myself was broken from the accumulation of events of the past few years. I had tried to find my way, making friends with the wrong people, falling in love with the wrong people, and believing in the wrong people and institutions.

I believed that, as Dad said, that I was useless without him. I had been wrong about so much. Dad convinced me that he was my only hope and that if I did everything he said, he could make up for all my mistakes. He made sure I knew he was the only reason I would amount to anything and my total obedience was the price.

This internship was more intense than the previous one, and things started going wrong right off the bat, but I didn't know any better. It was at a multinational energy corporation with decades of history and rated highly, Chevron. Something felt wrong in my gut, but I no longer trusted my instincts or my thoughts, so I did what they instructed me to do.

The company's strict hiring procedure required me to pass a drug test before I could be officially considered an intern. I knew I was going to pass the drug test, but I hadn't even scheduled my drug test yet when they asked me to begin work. This meant that I was not only working for free, but also unknowingly "working under the table". The person who was soon to be my supervisor, strongly insisted that work could not wait and started firing off tasks that he needed me to complete despite me not being recognized officially as an intern or being on payroll.

When I turned to Dad, Dad advised that I should work now despite not being paid as a gesture of goodwill to get on my soon-to-be supervisor's good side. Unreported employment is illegal employment, but I did not know anything about that at the time. I tried my best to complete the tasks given to me.

The tasks assigned to me while I was technically not an employee had not been too difficult. They had essentially asked me to research some travel options for flights and hotels for a group of their clients. After the drug test, and being officially added to their systems as an intern, work ramped up quickly.

I had mentioned on my resume that I was fluent in both Chinese and English. Although this was true, I expected that, as an intern, someone would still be checking my work. One time, I was asked to translate emails from English to Chinese that were going to be sent to top level executives. I was given only a few hours to complete this work. I was extremely stressed and worried I would mess up. I tried my best, but I was unfamiliar with business Chinese, which is far different from the Chinese I had studied in school. I handed in the emails by the deadline that afternoon. To my shock, not a single person checked my work and my translations were sent off to the top executives almost immediately.

The next day, I received a dressing-down from management. Apparently, I had mistranslated an honorary title that could either be indicative of top-level management or CEO. I had made my best guess that surely, they would not have a lowly intern drafting an email to a CEO, so I had typed in "top executive" where it should have said

"Chairman". I was berated for my mistake and told that it was my fault that the CEO of that company was now not replying to our Sales Director. I had bombed the relationship, or at least injured it. I was made to feel as though I was a complete failure and a waste of the internship position. The Sales Director shook his head in disgust.

As part of the intern program, us interns periodically spent time together and went on tours and various activities as part of training. Other interns seemed so happy and carefree. They described the boredom of doing easy or meaningless work, which was mostly just researching things to which their supervisors already knew the answers. Yet, here I was, submitting high visibility items with extremely challenging deadlines. It didn't seem fair or right.

Dad was unsympathetic and just flatly stated I was a useless art major and should be grateful for any opportunity and that I had better perform.

To make matters worse, there was a technical service engineer who took a fancy to me, inviting me over and over to coffee, lunch, or dinner. I refused all of these as politely as I could. He messaged me often via the company's internal chat program, interrupting my day with personal questions as he tried to get to know me. He was married and his baby was not even three months old yet, and he'd complain to me about his mother-in-law, his wife, and his new baby. My responses were curt and nearing the point of rudeness to discourage him. I tried to make him stop communicating with me, but my attempts failed.

Most employees had office mates, but mine was mostly out of town. Once this engineer found out that I could be cornered in my office alone quite easily, he came to visit me during work hours. There was no justification beyond him trying to see me. There was no connection between our work tasks.

He stood behind me as I tried to focus on doing work, but I could hear his breath too close to my skin as he looked over my shoulder to inquire what I was working on. I typed rapidly to hide my panic as his chin gently sank onto my shoulder. My whole body tensed; I hated this contact, but did not know what I could do to make it stop.

He was more senior than I was in the company. I was just an intern. The intern training had said to report these kinds of things but first, I thought to check with Dad. As an experienced executive, surely, he must be clear on what I should do.

Dad was against reporting. He told me it would land me in trouble and draw attention to me. He believed the engineer's advances to be harmless and meaningless. Both he and Mom criticized my lack of tolerance and waved off my extreme discomfort.

The engineer visited me frequently and I began crying at work and did my best to hide it, but one of the managers noticed my teary eyes one time when she checked in on "the new intern" to see how I was settling in. Since she was another woman and more senior within the company than the tech service engineer, I found myself breaking down when she asked if I was alright. I told her everything.

She had no tolerance for this kind of thing. Enraged, she dragged me in front of my supervisor, another manager, and the engineer's manager. We all sat down together and I repeated my story. The other managers were calmer and turned to the engineer's manager to hear her take on things.

She looked at me directly and explained that although it was unfortunate that I was distraught, she felt the best way to handle this situation was for her to tell the engineer to stop contacting or visiting me. The managers agreed that a report was a lot of paperwork and this could be easily resolved with a slap on the wrist.

After that, the engineer did stay away from me, so at least that was something. I had no idea if this was truly the correct solution or simply the easy solution for them. Perhaps it was both. I figured that if so many senior managers deemed the warning to be enough, then perhaps that was all that needed to be done. After all, what did I know?

* * *

MY WORKLOAD CONTINUED GROWING and I could barely think for all the projects I had going on at the same time. The majority of my work was related to marketing.

The marketing manager confessed to me she had hoped she would retire and take her full retirement package before internet became "a thing". As a result, the company was woefully behind in all marketing projects relating to internet or technology in general. I was asked to revamp every marketing project they had ever had.

By company metrics, my keyboard and mouse usage had far surpassed what was deemed acceptable and still, I was only barely meeting deadlines. I had to work many extra hours. My energy and health were used brutally to bring the marketing department up to speed.

I thought to talk to other interns about what I was experiencing in the hopes of understanding if what I was going through, was wrong. It definitely felt wrong, but the other interns proclaimed that I should take being overworked as a compliment. It meant that my supervisor trusted me, they said. I swallowed hard. That explanation did not make me feel better. Yet, there were so many intern voices to my one—perhaps I was wrong.

I relied more and more on caffeine to keep going, working through meals and nights to make deadlines, losing the precious pounds that I had put on so slowly and carefully just months before. I felt sick in my heart, mind, and body, but at least there was an end to the internship; it was only several months long after all.

I kept my tears private and soldiered to the end.

53

One good thing came out of the internship is that I met someone who sparked that warm, fuzzy feeling in my heart again. I fell in love with a mechanical engineer, Trevor. When he looked at me, his eyes sparkled and lit me up. I loved his hugs, his pillow-y shoulders, his chubby cheeks. I admired his work ethic and how respected he was in the company. He invited me out to tasty dinners and didn't demand kisses.

I was still plagued by panic attacks, although not as bad as I had been when I was with Soren. However, some days I would not feel safe to drive home immediately after the work day had ended. I would close the office door and curl up under my desk, hugging my knees tightly to my chest and struggle for air.

Trevor was there for me. He listened patiently and held me while I chokingly divulged to him a little bit about my past experiences. He would squeeze me tightly in his arms until my shuddering subsided and my harsh gasps subsided into quiet, calmer breaths so that I could drive home.

After a few dates, I initiated our first kiss, and loved the soft fuzz of his light facial hair brushing against the skin of my lips. He was warm and my heart glowed with life. We moved in together after just three months of dating. We went on many adventures, traveled internationally, and eventually, adopted two dogs together.

The dogs loved Monte far more than Monte was willing to reciprocate. They would try to lick Monte silly anytime they were given the chance. Monte learned to suffer their presence with grace and even accepted Trevor with minimal toe attacks. We were a family.

Our relationship was a huge step up for me from previous relationships, but it didn't come without its own challenges. Trevor had a long commute to work because of where we lived, so I had precious little time with him on weekdays. Understandably, he often just wanted to rest on weekends.

Once in a while, I did want to go somewhere and he was the kind of guy who liked to plan things. I learned that I needed to let him know a couple days or weeks in advance so he could research, make reservations, organize his work schedule and so forth for him to feel comfortable. At times though, his constant need for meticulous planning did put a strain on our relationship due to my desire for occasional spontaneity.

Trevor was the kind of guy who worked late or worked weekends sometimes. I admired his work ethic, but I also wished we had more time together. I tried to free up his time to hang out with me by taking on the majority of the cooking, cleaning, and other chores. This made him feel uncomfortable, he said. He felt I was being too much like a 60s wife, having dinner ready for when he came home, the house sparkling clean, dressing up for his return, and always asking about his day as he entered the door. His increasing guilt about not contributing as much in the relationship gnawed at him.

Once the MBA program began, I would text Trevor during the day between classes, and he usually wouldn't answer, later explaining that he was too busy. Sometimes, I felt lonely even though we were in a relationship together.

Although he wasn't good about texting, Trevor was great when he was present. We cuddled on the couch and watched movies or played games together. He took great care of me. He always could cheer me up if I was in a bad mood.

I preferred to drink warm water and he knew the perfect amount of hot and cold water to mix together for me to drink. No matter how tired he was, he would always wake up and help me if I had a bad nightmare or panic attack at night.

I felt guilty about robbing him of any amount of sleep though, so I resolved to begin counseling sessions again. I found a local mental health professional and began weekly therapy. I returned to the habit of reading self-help books and journaling for trauma.

Healing my mind was hard, but I continually kept at it. The new therapist asked me to bring out that long list of triggers, and we picked up where I had left off with the college therapist.

One-by-one, the therapist had me use mental exercises he taught me to desensitize myself. For example, since I feared being in close proximity with many men, he would ask me to meditate and focus on the feeling and image of me being in an elevator with all men who were taller and stronger than me. He asked me to imagine in as much detail as possible and helped me remain calm. Exercises like these taught my mind to not panic even though at first they were very painful for me.

It was extremely challenging, sessions often brought me to tears, but one by one, I did become less and less sensitive to my triggers.

54

Part of my healing, I decided, was that I needed to confront my fear of being attractive or sexy. And so, in the same vein of me doing ballroom dancing to brute force my fear of proximity with males and physical touch, I decided to do the same with "sexiness". And what better way than to sign up at a local fitness club that offered pole fitness lessons? Not only did I have to strip down to short, tight gym shorts and a sports bra, I also needed to be graceful and sexy.

Pole fitness was very challenging for many reasons; my physical strength was very low and my pain tolerance was even lower. Beginner grips such as pretending to sit in the air simply by holding one's body weight up off the ground and on the pole almost entirely using only thigh grip strength was foreign and challenging.

The pole was freezing cold against my skin. My skin would be stretched taut with the burning pain of my full body weight held up by just by my poor inner thigh skin that had never been subject to such usage before, all while trying to make everything look effortless and sexy.

In the class, we worked on developing strength, particularly in our core and upper body, flexibility, and pain tolerance. We swished our hair and learned to spin around the pole at dizzying speeds. I went often enough to make friends with other students. We'd support each other in class and laugh along with each other through our struggles.

My movements at first were very stiff and reluctant. I did not want to look sexy and yet was trying to look sexy in this class. While I battled internally, my muscles slowly developed, and my movements became a little smoother. While I still could not make my facial expressions appear relaxed and comfortable, at least I was able to get my body to move the way the instructor demonstrated.

Around Halloween time, the club had a tradition of having a performance night for students and instructors. Despite being new to pole fitness, to further challenge myself, I signed up to perform. I was only a few months into learning the baby steps of pole fitness, but I wanted to push myself to the next level of confronting my fear of sexiness. So far, I had been doing it in a somewhat private setting, a small class of only a few other women and myself in a closed space with no windows. Besides, I'd been too shy to show Trevor. He had never seen me dance and I wanted to excite him.

Over the next several weeks, I choreographed and practiced my amateur pole routine. The choreography I put together wasn't very challenging because I had a very short list of moves that I knew of or could do reliably. I playfully informed Trevor I intended to perform and of course, excitedly, he bought a ticket in advance to ensure he would have a seat in the audience.

I practiced and practiced, but I still felt it wasn't good enough. I tried to relax and focus on my main objective. The point for me was not so much to be the best pole dancing performer that night, but more to confront my fears. There was no doubt I was doing that in the biggest way I could think of.

As performance night approached, I started feeling cautiously optimistic about my ability to get through my routine. However, I received some bad news. Trevor had to go on a business trip. He would not be able to attend. My happiness was crushed, but I was not going to pull out of the performance because I still wanted to confront my fears. Being able to dance in front of him and excite him was a bonus that was now gone, but my resolution to perform did not waver. He left me his camera and tripod so that I could film the performance.

And so, Trevor took off on his business trip and I practiced the last few days before the performance. We were encouraged to dress up in Halloween costumes that allowed for safe and comfortable exercise. For lack of creativity, I decided to go with a kind of Cleopatra costume. I dressed in black shorts, a black sports bra, and bought a pair of large, Egyptian-themed earrings.

On the night of the performance, I tried to calm my nerves while the rest of the performers and audience members filed in. There was so much support from the community. Performers' friends and families rapidly filled all the seats and it warmed my heart to see so many people.

To my relief, my performance was one of the first shows of the evening. I wasn't going to be doing anything impressive compared to the other performers, and I'm was sure people would be confused why such a beginner would even choose to perform. Perhaps they'd think that I was some egomaniac who was eager to show-off. I was afraid I was making a fool of myself. I fretted while I waited backstage.

My teacher called for a round of applause to welcome me and queued to start the music. I walked out from behind the curtain and began my routine. The performance went by in a blur. Since I had practiced many times, the dance went smoothly. I did the whole routine to the best of my ability, and while I didn't consider it to be worthy of showcasing to others, the symbolic nature of it in terms of confronting one of my greatest fears was a major milestone for me.

I stopped going to classes shortly after that, since it was a bit of a commute. I bought a pole of my own though and, with Trevor's help, installed it in the garage. Although I practiced only seldom, it served as a mental reminder of this milestone; the pole represented that it was safe to be sexy. It felt good to feel sexy and powerful. And these were and are all major things marking my progress.

* * *

A MAJOR CHALLENGE FOR ME—and our relationship—was sexual intimacy. I hadn't been able to bring myself to talk to the therapist about this subject. He might have been able to help me with this, but I was far too uncomfortable talking about sex. Instead, Trevor and I tried to overcome this challenge by setting up symbolic actions so that I could signal if I was feeling panicky.

Simply saying "no" was impossible for me. I still have trouble saying that word in a sexual context, since Yi's treatment of me surfaces in my mind. I still remember the consequences in detail. With our system, I just had to squeeze Trevor's elbow. Onset of panic attacks often shut down my ability to verbally ask for help, so physical actions such as the elbow squeeze was how I communicated.

We also talked about how I should be the one to initiate sex, since Trevor was afraid of triggering me. I'm sure this made things a bit harder for him, because Trevor had a greater sexual appetite than I did. Although I'm sure he experienced sexual frustration from time to time, Trevor did not voice his complaints to me. I did not feel pressured to have sex, and this encouraged me to initiate with him more.

Life was good with Trevor. I wondered how long it would last. Should we be talking about marriage?

55

Even in my college years, Mom and Dad had been increasingly concerned about my future in terms of marriage. So, after dating and living with Trevor for some time, I felt that I should take him to meet the parents.

Trevor agreed with some reservation, because he had heard my descriptions of them. We made travel plans to China and I resolved to talk to Mom and Dad about marrying Trevor. I had never talked to Mom and Dad about marrying anyone. Thus, it wasn't until then that I learned about my arranged marriage.

I was ten years old when they first started playing with the idea of arranging a marriage for me. In his travels, Dad met many wealthy, successful people and their families.

One such family had a boy similar to my age and his parents asked if Dad might agree to a match. Dad half-jokingly agreed, giving a "we shall see" kind of answer. He felt it was a good match, as the family was quite wealthy and well-connected, which meant that I would live very comfortably. Technically, the traditional practice of arranged marriage is illegal in China; therefore, the most parents could do in this day and age was to have these loose verbal agreements which they then would try and talk their kids into.

Trevor was quite nervous having both never met Mom and Dad as well as visiting China for the first time. As a present, Dad gave us some coupons to use so that we could stay at one of the best hotels in Beijing for free, which I gladly accepted.

Shortly after checking in, Dad called and asked me to have a private dinner with a hotel owner's son. He explained that the family who owned the hotel we were staying at, were extremely wealthy and actually owned several expensive hotels throughout China. Dad told me the story of how I had met the son once when I was ten years old. I had no recollection of this meeting. Dad then explained how he had loosely agreed to arranging us at that time, and in thanks for the free hotel room, I ought to go to that dinner.

I pressed my cell phone to my ear as I sat on the bed across from Trevor, who was trying to quietly unpack our things to get us settled. It was very awkward.

Dad chatted as if Trevor didn't exist in my life. He claimed that if I went out with the hotel owner's son and we had a good connection, then I could have a wedding in this hotel. It would be one of the grandest weddings a girl could imagine. Dad seemed quite taken by this daydream.

Internally, I was laughing hysterically. Did he really think that I would swoon over the idea of a grand wedding with a stranger? Even if I were into weddings—which I was not—did he really think I'd make such a serious life decision based off of one lavish day? I felt that Dad didn't understand or know me at all. I took a deep breath and decided not to say any of that aloud; I merely quietly rejected Dad's dinner invitation.

I thought about hiding what Dad had just said to me on the phone from Trevor. I looked over at him as he carefully unpacked our clothes and toiletries. I ended up confiding in Trevor about the whole call and my reaction, because it was all so ridiculous and astounding to me. I was stunned and overwhelmed by all this information.

The trip went by in a blur. Although Trevor and I went to see several cultural and historical sites and took many pictures, I was preoccupied by how my parents were responding to him.

My parents were not impressed with Trevor. Behind his back, they would complain to me about his body weight and physical fitness. They felt that he was overweight and unmotivated about physical health. They stressed about how I would have to take care of him as he was destined for diabetes and would probably die before me.

My dad also criticized Trevor's position in the company, feeling that he was too low on the totem pole. Dad felt that both he and I could do better at finding me someone. There was also the language and cultural gulf. Trevor spoke no Chinese and although my parents spoke English just fine, they had strongly desired me to marry a Chinese man who appreciated the same values that they did. I knew they would never accept or like Trevor.

Trevor and I had somewhat expected this kind of outcome, so it was not a terrible shock. I was still disappointed, though. However, since it was still an international vacation with my beloved, we were able to enjoy ourselves traveling in China before we returned home.

56

Throughout the MBA program, I attended my classes and excelled in my studies, achieving a high GPA, higher than I had gotten in my undergraduate studies.

Some students wanted to be friends, but I didn't like what I saw in them. I was slightly disgusted by how many people gave themselves lofty titles to sound like a much bigger deal than they were. For example, one man was working for his Dad at a small shop that sold local, handmade jewelry. Since he fiddled with the internet there from time-to-time and there were no other employees, he titled himself "IT Director".

Another one of the students worked for Wells Fargo and boasted more than once about how he had been one of the people a few years ago selling subprime mortgages. This practice had been a large factor in the nationwide financial crisis. He laughed when he talked about how the bank had then switched him to the department that calls people to tell them they've lost their homes as a result of not being able to pay back the mortgage.

I kept everyone at arm's length, trying not to be too personable. I had filled my life with my hobbies and interests, studies, my pets, and my romance with Trevor; I didn't need anything to add to my boat.

I also didn't want to be used anymore, and that's often how I felt with others when it came to schoolwork. People would be friendly to me so they could get my notes or they wanted me to help them study, do their homework, or do all the group work.

I stuffed as many courses as I could into my schedule. As a result, a year and a half later, I graduated with a near 4.0 GPA. I refused to attend the graduation ceremony; I was just glad to be done with the MBA program and opted to have the school mail my diploma to me.

57

One of my favorite things to do with Trevor was just to lay still and cuddle. He was a great cuddler who wrapped his arms around me as I lay beside him. I'd put my ear over his chest and listen to his big heart thump-thumping away, his deep breathing, and feel the rumble of his words through his chest as he talked to me about subjects I couldn't care less about; I just loved hearing him speak.

Trevor loved Formula 1 racing and shared images of cars with me that I knew nothing of. I wanted to be supportive though, so sometimes I watched races on TV with him to keep him company. I loved snuggling with him on the couch to leech some of his body heat.

I brought up marriage on a random Tuesday and he guffawed at my spontaneity, knowing I was the kind of person who would leap about to whatever topic came to mind. He wanted to wait, but said he did want us to be together. Life as it was already felt like married life to me for the most part, anyways.

Life went on, and we were both comfortable in the security of our relationship. We even talked about buying a house together and looked at pictures online. Trevor wanted to buy a house closer to work, something by the water, something to call our own.

In spring, one of Trevor's childhood besties was getting married. We flew to Los Angeles to take part in the celebrations. Trevor was one of the groomsmen and I didn't know anyone else attending the wedding, so I was largely left to my own devices. I wandered around the empty reception area, taking pictures of the venue, of the staff preparing, and listening from outside to the bridesmaids' chatter through the windows of the building in which they were getting dressed. I watched the staff wheel out and set up chairs, tables, and decorations. After I got tired of taking pictures, I sat on a bench near the entrance and played cellphone games and read my Kindle, as I waited for the show to begin.

The wedding was beautiful, although I couldn't stop thinking about the money and work it must have taken to orchestrate everything. I whispered to Trevor that I would choose eloping over going through this whole circus, which made him laugh. It was all very pretty, but I would rather spend money on other things. After the vows and the after party was done, we returned to the hotel where everyone was staying.

Trevor had been up relatively early and we'd only just flown in the night before. He was tired and he could have gone to sleep in minutes, but I coaxed him into sitting up and dressing back in casual clothes. I expressed to him that this was one of those rare opportunities he could hang out with all his childhood besties and current good friends. They were all in their thirties, pursuing careers in different places, getting married, and starting families. I said he should go and hang out with the boys. We didn't know when we'd be in LA again, after all.

I assured him I would stay in the room so that he wouldn't have to worry about trying to involve me in the conversation. I figured they would have a lot of shared memories and inside jokes, and I didn't want to interrupt any of that. After thinking about it a minute, Trevor hugged me and thanked me for suggesting it.

He stripped out of his suit and pulled on a pair of comfy jeans and a t-shirt, kissed me on the forehead, and strode out the door. He had received a text saying that some of the guys were hanging out at the hotel lobby bar, so he joined them.

I curled up in the hotel bed, turned on the TV, and let that play in the background while I watched funny videos I'd recorded of Monte and the dogs on my phone. I already missed their furry little bodies, especially Monte's small round back pressed up against my legs while I slept. Hours passed, and I grew bored and sleepy. It was 2 am.

I texted Trevor to see what he was up to. I greatly enjoyed being tucked in at night. This was a nightly ritual between Trevor and I, and I was hoping he'd at least come upstairs for a few minutes to tuck me in before going back downstairs to hang out, but he didn't reply. After another thirty minutes of impatiently tossing and turning, I dragged on some clothes and wandered down the hall. Was the lobby bar even open anymore?

The elevator door opened with a soft ding, and I stepped into a silent lobby. The bar was closed, there were no guys, just a soft murmur of voices.

In the middle of the lobby, where there were some couches and seats, sat Trevor and one other person. A woman. They were cuddling on a couch, her head lying on his shoulder, their bodies completely pressed up against each other.

I felt a thunderbolt of calm surge through my body, and made my way as smoothly and solemnly as I could over to where they were. I sat adjacent to them in one of the chairs.

Trevor would not look at me and his cuddle partner was looking around everywhere for a place to escape. I was almost amused. The girl knew immediately that I felt their closeness was inappropriate, I think, but Trevor took several moments longer.

I knew him well enough to see what was going through his mind. On the one hand, he did not want to move away from his current position because that could mean admitting to guilt or wrongdoing. On the other hand, if he didn't move, then that wasn't particularly appropriate either. I was his girlfriend after all, and he hadn't even introduced me to this girl.

He eventually decided to remove his arm, and they awkwardly shifted away from each other. I chatted as if I had not seen anything, asking who the girl was, shaking her hand, inquiring where the other guys went. They stuttered out answers and couldn't agree on when the guys left.

The girl blurted out that she was waiting for her ride, a story that Trevor readily latched onto. However, when I quizzed them further on when this car was arriving, they had different answers again. Trevor thought it was ten to fifteen minutes, and the girl eventually admitted she hadn't even called for her ride yet.

She pulled out her phone and hurriedly punched in some numbers. She then insisted that since the driver had stated he would be there in less than ten minutes, that we could safely leave her in the lobby. I answered comfortably that we could all wait together for such a short period of time so that she wouldn't be alone in the lobby at 2:30ish in the morning. We all sat quietly and waited. Sure enough, the car pulled up after several minutes, but I'm sure they both felt it was an eternity. Trevor and I returned to the hotel room.

After the door had closed, I demanded an explanation of what had happened. His answer enraged me. Despite having been in a relationship with me for over two years now and having spoken of getting married, he used the excuse of "We haven't talked about the boundaries of our relationship and what you can and can't do, yet". He was defensive and insisted he had done nothing wrong, whereas I had a differing opinion. It was our first big fight. He ended up sleeping in the rental car. We eventually came to an agreement about what was appropriate and inappropriate.

Although I was very emotional and upset that night, after returning to our home, things seemed to go back to normal. I forgave him and asked only that he be sensitive to my hurt feelings in the short term.

58

Mom and Dad had been hounding me for nearly ten years to get blepharoplasty, an eyelid cosmetic surgery that was very common for Chinese people to get. People with double lids are considered to be highly attractive. My eyelids were naturally monolid and Mom and Dad wanted me to have the lid crease, or what was commonly referred to as double-lid.

I hadn't cared about it for a long time, but I had just started to experiment with makeup along with my pole fitness journey. Putting nice-looking makeup on monolids was a bit more challenging. So, for my vanity and makeup interest, the next time Dad offered to pay for this procedure, I accepted.

Together, Trevor and I attended the pre-surgery doctor appointment and consultation, we both knew the risks, knew the care-taking procedures, and had discussed how he would assist me in recovery. I would be largely blind for the first couple of days, and my eyelids would be swollen and painful. I would have to take pills and frequently ice my eyelids to lessen the pain and to speed my recovery. I would need him or someone to help care for me, because it would be difficult for me to open my eyes and see.

A month went by, and the surgery date was fast approaching. I became quite nervous. I'd never gone fully under before, and although

Trevor's brother was a doctor and they both kept emphasizing how I'd be fine, it still couldn't stop my nerves. I sought more comfort from Trevor as the surgery date approached, and he'd pet me gently and mumble everything would be ok.

Then Trevor's supervisor asked for someone on the team to fly overseas for a client on-site job in India. Eager to please his supervisor, I suppose, Trevor raised his hand despite knowing that the dates of the trip would coincide with my surgery. While he was in India, I would be alone and blind, helpless.

He called me around lunchtime to let me know, and I kept my voice normal as tears flowed down my face. He detected nothing wrong; it wasn't until he arrived home that he discovered my hurt feelings. And this time, there were no words, no amount of petting that could make it better.

I felt betrayed. I had been strongly depending on Trevor's promise to care for me after the surgery, yet now, he would be in India.

This was just a few short months from the cuddling incident. I could not reconcile the emotions I felt about his actions. I decided the relationship was over. I felt I couldn't depend on him in my time of need and how could I be with someone who I couldn't trust to be there for me?

* * *

I SUPPOSE I COULD HAVE broken up with him after I had recovered from the surgery, but I didn't want someone around who clearly cared so little for me. I initiated the break up, he moved out angrily, strongly believing that I was overreacting and offended that I would break up with him. Although I didn't agree with his opinion, I was thankful that he was not retaliatory and packed up swiftly.

The day came and I drove myself to the surgery, eyes red when the nurse asked me where my partner was or who would pick me up. I organized with a friend last minute to bring me home. I decided I would drive to the surgery, leave my car there and go pick up my car when I could see again. That parking lot there didn't have a rule against parking a car there too long anyways, and the clinic was only a thirty-minute walk home.

They put me under, and the next thing I knew, I had woken up, I was propped up to be sitting almost upright, and I could not open my eyes.

I could not open them.

[NO!]

My eyelids refused to move. Fearing the worst, I began to panic, my heartrate sky rocketed, and my breathing sounded harsh in my own ears. A nurse rushed in and hurriedly tried to soothe me, dabbing at my eyes deftly. She explained that it was just some dried blood gluing my eyes shut and if I relaxed, she could dab it all away.

Under her breath, I heard her mutter that I wasn't supposed to be awake quite yet. She warned me that if I did not calm down, I could really hurt myself. I gulped down my hysteria, remembering exercises from books and therapy.

The surgeon and the nurse congratulated me together that the surgery had been very successful. I was able to crack open my gummy eyelids with some effort, and could see they were all smiles. I was cleaned up and wheeled out to the lobby where my friend, Anne, would take over. Anne helped me into her car and drove me home.

She hung out for several hours, helping me microwave a meal and changing out ice packs for my eyes as I lay helplessly in a recliner. We chatted at length and then she had to go home to her husband. After she left and the silence of the house descended on me, I wondered if I'd made a mistake. I had no way to really distract myself now from thoughts of the breakup of just days ago.

The nurse had emphasized how I must not cry because if I sobbed too hard, it could rip open the sutures. I would not only hurt, but also could scar terribly, which would most certainly require a correctional procedure. I willed myself to be composed, employing all the emotion mastery techniques I had learned in therapy, but my broken heart was stronger. The drugs they gave me made me feel loopy, my eyelids pulsed with incessant pain, sleep was difficult, and I missed my tuck-ins. I cried.

Mom and Dad randomly called me on video chat to check in on me. I hadn't told them I was doing the surgery as I wanted to surprise them. When I picked up the phone and they saw my face they were shocked, happy, and concerned.

During the call the topic of Trevor came up. Between everything that was going on, physical and emotional changes, perhaps drugs, perhaps the uncertainty of my future once again since I'd just finished my MBA by then and was unsure about what lay ahead, perhaps coupled with the silence of the house, and my pets' anxious whining since I couldn't walk them, I simply couldn't keep my emotions in check. For the first time in many years, Mom and Dad saw me cry.

They were thunderstruck, since they both hardly saw me display emotion anymore. To their credit, they quickly bought plane tickets to come care for me. Dad asked for time off from work and arrived at my door a couple days later.

Dad helped walk the dogs, and Mom helped cook food since I had only been able to reheat food I'd cooked in preparation, or make instant ramen. She researched and cooked extra nutritious meals so that my body could recover from the trauma of it all. Probably because my emotional state was not amazing, the recovery took a little longer than the average length the nurses had described. Surprisingly, Mom and Dad were too busy rejoicing over the surgery and breakup with Trevor to be insulting towards me. After I could see again, they returned to China.

I love my new eyelids, despite the slight scarring I have from inevitably ripping the sutures a bit during the healing process. Applying color to them became more fun, and other fun makeup looks were now available to me, too. Once the skin wasn't so tender, I bought an eyeshadow palette of all sorts of colors, a few pencils and liquid liners, and my face became another canvas for me to paint on occasionally. With a little makeup, I can't even see the scars.

59

Some months went by and I worked on finding a job. In my free time, I still played computer games. I felt online was a safe, controlled way to talk with people. If anyone hurt me or caused me stress, I could easily delete them from my friends list. Everyone was replaceable, and I was in control.

It was through games that I met my next love, Joe. Joe was deployed in South Korea; an air force man, tall and handsome. We were the same age.

I started flirting with him, playing with him more and more. We started having frequent phone calls and video chats. I felt it was perfect; with the physical distance between us, I could be in love and not risk any hurt to my body. With the time difference, I could work on my job and various hobbies uninterrupted. We would talk at night, which was his lunch break. Joe had a soft voice and I enjoyed hearing him chuckle and cuss creatively in mock-rage at the games we played.

Several months went by. He ended his seven years of service in the US Air Force to become a college student at a school near to me, moved in with me, and started classes soon after.

He periodically received payments through the GI Bill to support his studies. We had the usual couple's squabbles over house chores and lifestyle adjustments, but we adapted to each other smoothly overall. He was everything Trevor had been and more. He would text me during the day, even when he was on campus and I'd never had such attention.

I basked in the luxury of it, drinking it in greedily.

60

I received a job offer at Chevron, the same place at which I'd interned and where that one married engineer with the new baby had harassed me.

Mom and Dad snarled at me to quit being such a baby, to quit being so weak that I could not handle a little bit of harassment. They insisted that it was a great company and that I was being a spoiled brat. They'd rail on and on about how it was just my fault; I needed to work on how I dressed or interacted with people at work, and so on.

Things started going sour before I started working. My supervisor from before called me in to talk about my duties as part of the pre-start-date meetings.

I came prepared to talk about my resume, school, and work-related achievements. To my surprise, he didn't want to talk about duties and responsibilities. Instead, he brought up the harasser I had reported to management as an intern, warning me sternly not to do so again. He added that I couldn't be trusted to be an employee under him if I was going to be a troublemaker. Dad had been right. I had a black mark on my record.

He asked if I could give him some sort of guarantee that I had learned from the past. He was a busy man and didn't have time to handle a young girl and her drama. I was taken aback and shocked by this subject matter. I ended up stammering out some sort of reply along the lines of I did not feel that this was going to be a repeat event. I explained how it was not my fault that the other engineer had harassed me, but my soon-to-be-supervisor seemed disinterested in my reply and waved me to a halt.

When I started work, I learned that this supervisor had given me to his subordinate for reporting. The result of this made it so that he could assign me work without having to deal with any paperwork related to me. His subordinate had work that he wanted done, too, and since the President of that branch had heard my name bandied about as the new marketing person, even he handed me a project here and there.

Managing three bosses who were in direct reporting line of each other was very challenging. Not wanting to disappoint or snub anyone, I felt I could refuse no one.

I was rapidly turning twenty-six and could no longer be on my Dad's health insurance policy. Therefore, in the first month of working, I made sure to research medical, dental, and mental health related benefits to understand co-payments and so on. I wasted no time and called several therapists who were on the list and in a nearby location to where I lived. I looked specifically for therapists who had experience working with patients with sexual abuse and relationship issues. I called and left voicemails, since most therapists were not accepting new patients.

I started to feel anxious that I would not find someone soon. Despite it only being my first month on the job, I was already desperate for therapy to support me. That probably should have been a major red flag.

After calling multiple locations, one lady finally called me back. She was the first one to call me back and schedule a time, and I took the time slot immediately.

She was an elderly lady who was full of life and cheer, strong instincts, and deep wisdom. I showed up to the first session full of nerves, unsure of how things would go. I really needed a good therapist right now. I also had not yet bonded deeply with any of the therapists I had seen on and off for a long time. I don't even remember their names.

But this time was different. This therapist turned into the only one who's name I have remembered.

Her name was Mindy. Sessions with Mindy were very tough. Our first several sessions were about going through the timeline of my life; talking on a high level about all the painful things I had experienced. The struggle was that by this time, it took ages to get through a high-level summary of my tumultuous past. Furthermore, because there was so much going on each week at work, it was hard to find time to talk about the past as I was full of fears and concerns about the present.

My new manager mentioned to me the first month that my predecessor in the marketing position had passed away suddenly the year prior, so there would be no knowledge transfer, and they desperately needed work done in marketing. It was the lady who had helped me report my harasser from before and I was sad that she was gone.

My workload exploded soon after the first month. This arm of the company was asked to cut a large percentage of employees. Looking at my resume, management hoped I would replace the contractors that they had hired to assist my predecessor. All the previous contractors were laid off within the first year of me being on the job. Suddenly, I was made marketing director, market analyst, occasional translator, web designer, graphics designer, social marketing manager, event coordinator, hospitality manager, content writer, video marketing editor, videographer, and communications specialist. I was an entire marketing department in one person.

I also picked up a new harasser. He bumped into me while I was leaving the parking garage one morning. He struck up a polite conversation as we both walked towards the office building and, not wanting to be rude, I obliged in responding to the small talk. He explained he'd heard of me through the usual "Welcome New Employee" email that was blasted to everyone.

Soon after, he started messaging me on the company internal chat program frequently. He'd prattle on and on about how often he worked out, his hobbies—that sort of thing. I could care less. I didn't know his rank or position, and I didn't know if I could afford to be rude and block him. I was barely polite in tone with my monosyllabic replies.

It didn't matter. He seemed perfectly happy to chat on and on about himself. He boldly asked me one day what time I usually arrived at work in the mornings, when I usually left, the make and model of my vehicle, and what floor of the parking garage I parked on. Alarmed, I asked him why he wanted to know that, and he confessed to me it was because he wanted to be able to wait for me there, or accompany me to my car.

He tried to schedule meetings with me although there was no reason for us to be working together. We were assigned to entirely different products in the company and he was not in a position to be dictating any marketing projects anyways. I knew he was just trying to find a reason to be with me, so I started filling my calendar up with fake meetings.

I begged the IT department to allow me to manually set "away" or "online" statuses. They were defaulted to being automatic, so he would know when I left my desk, and I was afraid after he mentioned this a few times. IT sympathized, but they unfortunately could not change these corporate directed settings, so I turned to the security staff. I asked them where the cameras were, so I made sure to park there every morning, changing floors ever so often, and changed my schedule to get to work at different times.

I kept it up for two months. He had mentioned he was being transferred to another location after that. After he left, I relaxed enough to breathe. I felt triumphant. I hadn't reported him and he was out of my hair now. He still tried emailing me after his transfer, but these were easy to ignore since he was now in another country. I felt good that I'd taken care of this by myself.

* * *

OTHER THAN HARASSMENT AND WORKLOAD, the commute was not anything to sneeze at either. I would drive one and a half hours to work starting at about six in the morning, and then drive one and a half hours back late afternoon or evening. Because of the workload, I often had to stay late. My supervisor would state very clearly that if I had to take care of this or that by tonight, no matter what it took, I had to "make it happen". So, I would.

Trevor had not wanted anything to do with the pets when he moved out, so I was now juggling the new job while still caring for the two dogs and Monte. I put the dogs into doggie daycare, dropping them off and picking them up every day so that they wouldn't be alone for so many hours. They seemed happy every time I picked them up from the daycare and slept peacefully through the night. I was grateful, I had no energy left for them at the end of the work days. I would feed them, force some food into my body, and collapse into a mindless zombie state, doing nothing, then going to sleep, starting the next day. Despite how exhausted I was, I squeezed in time for sessions with Mindy, needing her support more and more.

Life was insanity from amount of workload alone and unfortunately, after getting rid of that one harasser, more showed up. Between that and dealing with three levels of management and the politics that came with it, I felt on the verge of a breakdown.

I lost weight, I cried at work, my panic attacks came back in force. I was falling apart. Going out on a limb, I confided in my supervisor that I was losing weight from the stress and overwork. He vocalized sympathies to me, and promised to see what he could do. The next day, he added more work. This happened each time I complained about my workload. After a couple times, I learned to stop screwing myself over further. I learned not to show weakness around him. It would only make things worse.

Despite everything—and to my great surprise—my projects and results were well received. I received compliments from the higher-ups and our clients. Although this was great, it also made my peers insanely jealous. I would receive barbed messages from my supervisor and peers—in person and in email—about how I was not good at all and it was only because my dad had influenced everyone to give me a position I didn't deserve.

One time, my supervisor claimed that when his boss, the director, had complimented me, he was just lying to my face. My supervisor insisted that only he knew what the director really thought, and that I shouldn't trust my own observations. He assured me that the director felt that my designated tasks were worthless and was merely trying to be nice.

One day, my supervisor had some contract issues to work out with a manufacturer of refinery parts for the technology that our department licensed. Our director wanted logos stamped on the refinery parts, which was not as simple as one might think. My supervisor tasked me with the project and so I interviewed the head mechanical engineer who had designed the parts.

The parts would be subject to extremely high temperatures and chemical treatments due to being used to process crude oil. The parts would not usually be visible. My first challenge was to find out where and how to place a visible logo on these giant metal pieces. Location had to be carefully chosen because depending on the location, a logo could easily be blasted off in the first run cycle.

For years, the legal team had strongly encouraged the company to include logos on each piece, but it wasn't until I had joined the team that they decided to push this project. My supervisor hounded me extremely hard on this project and wanted me to solve the problem immediately. He required me to solve the issue in just a few short weeks, despite management previously allowing this issue to fester for decades. I had never dealt with this particular issue before and did my best to go about it as professionally as possible.

After I had discussed and settled on an appropriate logo size with the design team, I spoke with the manufacturers. It took several meetings to devise a way for all parties to be satisfied with logo placement. Each manager I spoke to had different concerns and I had taken into consideration cost, time, and legal aspects. We tried to find the best, easiest, and cheapest way to include the logo without delaying delivery to our clients.

I'm not sure if I was actually expected to meet this challenging deadline or if I was meant to fail from the outset. It took a lot of working overtime and talking to people in different time zones, but I finally completed the job, despite the complexity of the task.

I thought my supervisor would be pleased, but if anything, he seemed angrier after this project. He would occasionally rage about how slow I was about work. Sometimes, he would pressure me to take shortcuts I wasn't willing to take, simply so that he could proudly report to his supervisor that the job was finished.

Despite his temper, I stuck to my guns and made sure to complete my work projects to a high standard. After all, it was preached that the "Chevron Way" was about pursuing "disciplined operational excellence".

I was confused by his clear departure from several core company culture values. Dad said to ignore my supervisor and stick to the

"Chevron Way" because my supervisor might have been trying to set me up to look bad. With Dad's warning, I worked even more carefully than before.

* * *

I STRUGGLED TO UNDERSTAND how to make my supervisor happy. Half kidding, I babbled that, as a recent graduate, what if we talked about quality of work in terms of grades. I asked him directly what grade he wanted in terms of my assignments and how he graded what I had been doing. He admitted he felt I was doing A-grade quality work, but that it took too long, and that A's were entirely unnecessary. He wanted C-grade work just get the job done. He explained that my workload was my own fault, because I insisted on having these stupidly high standards. Furthermore, he threatened to continue taking away time, other resources, or people from me in order to force me to a do the work faster than I was.

Mom and Dad wouldn't hear any of my complaints about my work environment, discrediting any of my feelings by hissing it was the first job and I had no idea what things were like elsewhere. They promised me that other companies would have worse working conditions, and reminded me that this was an award-winning Fortune 500 company after all. They emphasized that I either needed to toughen up or give up and marry someone they found for me.

I grit my teeth, but what could I say? What did I know? What if things actually were a lot worse elsewhere?

Maybe they were right. Chevron truly did have many rewards, such as the Catalyst Award for its Chevron Way: Engineering Opportunities for Women initiative and an award for companies committed to the recruitment, development, and advancement of women, or the Global Healthy Workplace Award, Corporate Equality Index Award, the list went on and on. In my mind, these awards must mean something, and if I couldn't handle it here, perhaps I couldn't handle it elsewhere either. Besides, if I quit the job, the repercussions would be unfathomable. Not only would I have no income, no healthcare, and no more sessions with Mindy, I would also most definitely experience Mom and Dad's ire and abuse.

Miraculously, I continued to perform at work. The company used my advertisements internationally and these earned high marks and praise. We scored top 10 for all surveyed categories, which were tested by third-party sources, beating departments and competitors in our niche that had much larger teams and much higher marketing budgets than we had. It was also the first time in our department's history to have been in the top 10.

I didn't have time to relax or feel proud. The company website hadn't been updated since its creation in the 90s. I designed, developed, and created content for all our needs. I attended a multitude of conferences and even hosted my first ever hospitality suite. It was for the largest annual technical summit and my suite was praised as one of the most memorable and beautiful ones. We had many visitors and our sales team had no shortage of potential clients to talk to.

My health continued to deteriorate under the massive workload and stress. Maybe the manager knew this, or he was engineering it on purpose. I noticed him isolating me from my colleagues. One time, he put an arm across the meeting room door as I was about to enter, explaining I didn't need to attend these sales meetings and that there were better usages of my time.

I had been attending these meetings as a way to understand how our technologies worked, find out what clients found most valuable, and to get to know more people in the company. After all, my previous internship, my MBA, and my undergraduate degree had not educated me about anything related to the work I was doing now. In public, my supervisor praised me, his newest employee, for getting along with everyone, but in private, he strongly discouraged me from speaking to other employees in our building, commenting that I was getting too close to certain "nobodies" in other departments and wasting my time.

It was from one of the "nobody" connections I made in a meeting that I learned a dark secret. A senior member of the company told me my predecessor had not simply passed away, but she had actually committed suicide by jumping off the Golden Gate Bridge. This revelation sent a chill down my spine.

My supervisor criticized my mental capacity frequently, claiming that I had serious focus issues. He explained that he was trying to train me to learn his way of thinking, and his standards, because only then, things would be ok. He expressed confidence that I would continue to suffer until I saw his way of things. Sometimes, he would gaslight me by accusing me of deleting an email he had sent or forgetting something he had told me on the phone when I was sure that none of that had happened.

His gaslighting eventually wore down my sanity and I began to believe him when he said that I had mental problems. Not even rape and sexual abuse had caused me to turn to using prescription drugs, but for the first time, I felt it was necessary. I sought out a psychologist through my healthcare plan and received my first prescription for mental health related drugs.

Between the drugs, Mindy, and the coping mechanisms I had learned in previous books and seminars, some months passed. I continued to work as best as I could.

61

I tried to compensate for the negativity at work by being happy in other aspects of life. I had always enjoyed learning, so I turned to education once more as a coping mechanism. As a result, I started learning about investing and 401Ks, savings, returns, America's credit score system, and tax optimization. This was new territory for me, but I enjoyed learning about all this financial stuff. I read a lot of nonfiction books. Several of them inspired me to take action to improve my financial future.

Reading *Rich Dad, Poor Dad* by Robert Kiyosaki inspired me to enter into real estate. I decided to buy my own house. A month from my twenty-seventh birthday, I purchased my first home. This not only cut down my three-hour work commute, but also made me feel tremendously grown-up. Plus, I had new homeowner pride.

My new house was only fifteen minutes from work and thus, I wound up going home each day for lunch. It was easier to hide my tears at home than at work. Despite the happiness the house bought me, I cried almost every day. My supervisor cruelly gave me two additional email inboxes to manage and casually mentioned that this year was actually a quiet year for the department; it was projected that next year would be much busier.

Nearing the end of my rope, I began to seek out a variety of solutions to make work life more bearable. I even reached out to upper management. I still wanted to trust that the company's awards and oft-quoted values might protect me.

I was wrong. The senior manager I confided in smiled at my tear-stained face and advised me that my challenges with my supervisor were a fantastic opportunity to practice my influence. I should try learning to influence my manager. The senior manager was adamant that all new, young employees should learn such skills and waxed on about his back-in-the-days. I didn't reach out to him again.

One of the problems with this new house was that although the commute was shorter, I was now much too far away from Mindy to have sessions. I tried to keep it up for several more weeks, but the drive was just too much. I ended sessions with Mindy. I didn't have the energy to develop a new relationship with a new therapist.

I changed many of my behaviors in hopes of protecting myself. I was careful in how I talked with others, avoiding closed door talks as much as possible, and dressing extremely conservatively.

I struggled with my external appearance. On the one hand, I wanted to look put-together and professional. On the other hand, I believed that perhaps because of my external appearance, I attracted unwanted attention.

I felt guilt and shame for being harassed. I felt that it was my fault given what Mom and Dad were saying. I avoided wearing skirts or heels at work, changed my wardrobe to long full pants and plain, close-toed flats. I wore a coat or a vest when I wore a blouse. Other times, I wore turtlenecks to cover as much skin as possible. I stuck to sports bras so that my chest would not move and would be squashed down so as to look flatter.

But still, I was sexually harassed. One time, I wore a purple vest over a black turtleneck, full pants, and my flats. I sat at my desk, quietly typing up some emails.

An older man worked on my floor in the sales team as a Senior Account Manager. He was in his 60s, short, and had scruffy mustache. Innocently, he toddled over to my desk. I politely greeted him and asked how he was doing. He explained he didn't have any business to discuss with me, but wanted to compliment my purple vest. I was puzzled and surprised, but thanked him anyway.

Unprompted, he shared that his favorite color was purple, even going a step further crooning, "I hope you don't mind if I admire it a while longer".

He motioned for me to keep working while he stared directly at my chest. I was speechless; my fingers rested motionless over my keyboard. I could not believe how blatantly he was ogling me. I had seen him in the coffee room a few times before, and noticed him looking, but had always told myself that it was just my imagination. I felt powerless. I doubted staring was a reportable offense. I would just be told I was a drama queen and troublemaker again.

I felt terrible. Dad was too annoyed to listen to my complaints this time, and told me if I was so committed to ruining my career, I should go irritate my supervisor. Although I had reservations about going to my supervisor, I had a naive hope that perhaps—at least on this one subject—he might act as a supervisor should and protect his underling.

I was wrong again. He snickered at my story, pointing to the fact that my colleague was short enough that his eyes were right at my chest level. After a good laugh, my supervisor mentioned that even if the Senior Account Manager had been staring at my chest all those times, the man was a year or two from retirement age anyways.

My supervisor waved me back to my office and insisted it wasn't worth it to start any trouble. After all, it wasn't that bad to get stared at, so he implored me to just try and bear it. It wasn't like the Account

Manager was physically hurting or touching me, and therefore, it wasn't that big of a deal.

I was confused, but also partially believed what my supervisor had said. After all, with all that management training, surely my supervisor knew what was best for this situation, shouldn't he?

I reached out to Mom and Dad again for their opinion. Dad said I should listen to Mom and Mom clearly sided with my supervisor. She snorted derisively at my complaints, echoing my supervisor's comments. She snapped at me to stop fussing about it and focus on the important things at work.

I felt that I was one voice against many, and although it didn't feel good I wasn't sure what I could or should do. Everyone who had lived longer than me and had more experience than I had at handling these things was telling me to just shut up about it. Surely, they knew better than I did. I thought they must be right. Maybe I was too sensitive or unreasonable, just as they were telling me I was.

I tried to be satisfied in trusting their opinions. I tried my best to deal with everything. I never confronted the account manager. I didn't bring it up again to my supervisor. I focused all my energy on working and coping.

62

I was able to keep it together for another few months, but severe depression and burnout was inevitable. I lost another ten pounds and my ribs started to show. In desperation, I reached out to the Employee Conflict Group. Unlike HR, things were not automatically reported and documented. My understanding was that the help they could give was kind of half HR-ish and half counseling-ish.

I was put in contact with a kind lady there who reminded me in some ways of Mindy. She was sympathetic to my distress, but unfortunately, could not give me any good news. In fact, she confided that from what she knew of the department I worked in, her best advice was to change departments or change companies. She encouraged me to use sick days to rest and recover.

I felt hopeless and began using the sick days I had until I was all out. I didn't have many of them to start with, seeing as I was a new employee. The lady from Employee Conflict Group referred me to a new therapist. She suggested that I take advantage of my option of taking medical leave and schedule many sessions for my mental health.

After a particularly brutal week of working over one hundred and twenty hours, I dragged myself to work the following Monday, feeling extremely worn down after meeting another crazy deadline. To my surprise, my supervisor threatened to fire me.

He added another project to my pile and I had quietly, but firmly, asked for a much later deadline than what he had suggested. I listed all the other work he had me doing currently and how it would not be plausible to complete all the other deadlines if I were to accept his proposed deadline.

Furthermore, even if my plate were completely empty, I had no confidence in my ability to complete this new project by the time he wanted me to have it. I asked him to shuffle his prioritization of my workload if this new task was so imperative, and to hear me out on a reasonable deadline.

He exploded in rage, calling me insubordinate, threatening to replace me, slamming a table with a big, meaty fist. I let him finish his tirade, asked that we speak about this project another time, and excused myself.

I met with the therapist the next day and she immediately put me out on medical leave.

* * *

I BREATHED. I finally had the time and energy to put some attention on my relationship with Joe and on my house. Cleaning up and organizing the house felt therapeutic. Going on dates and playing games with Joe filled me with happiness. But all was not well with Joe, either.

Turned out he was skipping classes, and complaining about frequent migraines. I had a difficult time understanding this. He had admitted that he'd had migraines while he was in military as well, but still consistently made it to work every day. He skipped enough classes and slacked enough on doing schoolwork that he started having to drop out of classes to avoid Fs on his record.

I urged him to ask his professors for extra credit projects to salvage what he could of his GPA. I tried to assist him, but Joe was determined to do school on his terms, refusing any of my help. He declared he wanted to see what he could accomplish on his own.

And it didn't stop there. Other than his academic troubles, Joe also had a bad spending habit. He spent everything he had and more. His credit had been excellent, so his credit card limit was such that the balance could be blasted up to over $15k, and he ran it up, all the way.

Joe had no job, was not searching for one, and really had no way to pay it all off. Yet still, he kept purchasing what he wanted, when he wanted. I had not asked in too much detail about how his pay from his military service worked and therefore had not known he was spending so much more than he had coming in. Even if I had, I felt that it was his responsibility as an adult to be budgeting and managing his financial situation. I was not his mother and we were not married.

I was appalled on his behalf over the amount of interest he would have to pay on such a large amount of credit debt, but also hurt by a sense of financial betrayal. Because Joe hadn't managed his money well, he admitted that he could no longer to afford his portion of our living costs. Our original agreement was that we would split living expenses except for furniture which I paid for in full. Since he couldn't carry his own financial weight in our relationship, this meant that I would have more on my plate.

I was angry. If he had been open about his financial situation and spending habits, we could have perhaps done something about his debt before it had ballooned to over $15,000. It was overwhelming.

Since I was in a financial situation where I could afford to loan him the money he needed to pay off this debt, I felt obligated to help him. I loved him and I knew no one in his family were in a position to assist in this way. I had reservations though, because I had never lent money to anyone before and I wasn't sure if he could be trusted with such a large sum. To protect myself, I did some quick research online and drafted up a loan document in the event that he refused to pay me back. He signed, I transferred the funds, and the credit card debt was gone. I breathed again.

* * *

RELIEF WAS ONLY SHORT-LIVED THOUGH, because having him owe me so much money wore down on the relationship terribly. Every time he made some other frivolous purchase, it eroded my feelings for him. I couldn't stop myself from nagging him about his expenditures. For example, I would criticize him for spoiling himself with a new gym bag or towels when we had perfectly good gym bags and towels already. Joe also had a vaping habit and would spend money he didn't have to buy the juices to fill his vape and frequently upgrade his vape kit. I felt that the upgrades and the pricier juices were an unnecessary expense.

As a gamer, I periodically upgraded my computer to keep up with how demanding newer games were on computer hardware. Now that I was on medical leave and could actually play more and think about which pieces to upgrade, I did a little shopping therapy for myself. However, when I went and upgraded my computer, Joe wanted to upgrade his computer as well. The computer parts were not cheap. I didn't have the energy to stop him—not that I could have—so, I despaired.

I escaped through games, playing most hours of the day to avoid thinking about anything stressful. I wore pajamas most days, avoided going outside, and set very low, easy daily goals. I tried to focus on just eating and drinking.

I went back to reading self-help and improvement books. I cleaned and organized the house as though it would fix all of our relationship problems. In reality, we were arguing more and more. I wanted him to do better in school and told him the importance of not having high credit card debt. I tried to help him set up a budget plan. And over all this, work stress still loomed over me like a dark cloud that wouldn't go away. Days passed, weeks passed.

Joe started developing some anger issues, probably because he was frustrated with his school and financial crisis as well as my criticisms anytime he made what I believed to be a frivolous purchase. On my end I too felt more and more frustrated. I was supposed to be home on medical leave; the idea was to get better by being away from work, but I felt unable to heal at home either. It became clear we were no good for each other. I was not sure how much longer the relationship would last. I did not have the energy to work on everything.

I found my limit the next time he confessed the truth to me about his credit card statement. He was another $10,000 in debt somehow. Exhausted, disappointed, and depressed, I asked for us to end the relationship, and he nodded wearily as well. So, we split, quietly; no fighting, no rage, just relief that it was over.

We were just roommates for another month before he could figure out his next steps. He ended up moving cross country to be with his soon-to-be retiring dad. He sent most of his things with a moving truck and the rest in his car, which he drove back home to Florida.

We tried to be at least online friends for a while but I continued to be unhappy with the ongoing loan contract between us. This was made worse by the fact that he would discuss with me his dreams of purchasing a house and other large expenditures when he had already missed our mutually agreed upon date to pay me back. I felt highly irritated that he didn't seem to appreciate what I had done for him or respect our loan agreement and deadline. He promised to pay back the amount he owed, but it was hard for me to trust him anymore. In the end, he did make some partial payments. In an effort to reduce stress and negative reminders in my life, I decided I could not have a relationship as friends with him after all, and deleted him online.

And just like that he was gone from my life.

63

Shortly after Joe and I separated, my medical leave ran out. When I returned to work, I was informed that the public story was that I burned myself out by working too hard. Management told me that this story was harmless. They felt it was okay for employees to burn out from working so hard for the company. This would save face for everyone—and by everyone, they meant my boss.

My reporting hierarchy was changed temporarily to someone else while management figured out what to do with me. My supervisor was still allowed to assign work to me, but he now had to do so by asking his boss to communicate that to me. I hoped things would change for the better.

To my despair, my workload was heavier than before. Anything I had been working on had simply been neglected the entire time I was gone. I scrambled through the literally thousands of emails that had piled up.

Sometimes I'd still have to interact with my old boss, and he was passive aggressive at best, even via email. One time, he tried to make me search for someone's email address through the phone directory, giving me their first name only. The phone directory was alphabetically ordered by last name.

The old phone directory had never been converted into an electronic version. My old supervisor was well aware that this would cause me needless struggles. He had this individual's email and knew his last name. I'm sure he was grinning in his office imagining me poring over the phone directory pages, reading every name.

I did not have time to play this game and did not want to be his plaything anymore. There were a lot of old-timers who were well connected on my floor and knew almost everyone. I figured it would be faster just to ask someone. I went down the hall knocking on doors asking who knew the contact info I needed.

When they asked why I was looking for this person, I truthfully explained that my old supervisor had asked me to perform this task, but only told me the first name. My old supervisor apparently had a reputation of being mean and petty it seemed, so there were some head shakes and eye rolls on my behalf and eventually, someone was able to provide the full name and email address I needed.

Emboldened by sessions with my therapist, I felt strong enough to approach upper management and tell them the truth of what had transpired. I felt that it was important for them to know. Surely, they would care about what my old supervisor—their underling—was doing. Surely, they would care about a manager asking employees to do poor quality work. Surely, they would care about a manager torturing an employee. Surely, they would do something.

After hearing me out, upper management said that if what I had described was true, my manager's behavior was indeed unacceptable and that an investigation should be launched. However, out of the group, my boss' supervisor spoke up and flatly stated that I was not to be believed. He said I wasn't credible from an age and experience standpoint.

He pointed out how my supervisor had been with the company much longer than I had been. He then turned to me and said, "I'm sorry your personal perception and version of events has caused you such distress; that and that alone I believe to be real". My case was dismissed before any investigation occurred.

I was labelled a liar to get them out of having to launch an actual investigation. Even though I knew that I had not lied about anything, I felt deeply humiliated and outraged about what had happened.

I felt that my next choice was very clear. I handed in my resignation, finished my last project, and packed up. The senior director who had spoken up in the meeting, escorted me out of the building. He didn't offer extend courtesy handshake and neither did I.

* * *

FRIENDS WITHIN THE COMPANY told me that I could consider legal action. Some were also angry on my behalf. Older employees sympathized, but told me this kind of thing sometimes happens. Younger employees who had not yet been worn down by injustice in the world raged with me.

I felt that I needed to make at least one more effort to right the wrong that had been done to me, so I scheduled some consultations with lawyers to hear their professional opinion. A couple of them sympathized, but most threw up their hands.

One of them stated that the Conflict Resolution department had manipulated me into ruining my case when I agreed to go on medical leave. They believed that this could and would be used against me. Furthermore, since I didn't have recordings of the conversations, it was impossible to prove anything.

He added that the company could call other employees to testify and they would, of course, support the company. Not only that, but I would be buried in legal fees long before it reached that stage. Another lawyer noted that the jurisdiction that would get a jury for such a case was very pro-business, which meant that a jury would most likely side with a company as opposed to an individual.

In the unlikely case that I even succeeded, Dad still worked for Chevron. Mom and Dad strongly discouraged me from proceeding with a suit, claiming it could hurt Dad's job. Now that I was unemployed, I would need his help more than ever.

I was also informed that if I went through with this case—win or lose—it would be a huge, black mark on my employment record. Future employers would know that I was a troublemaker. It would hurt my chances at being employed anywhere.

Furthermore, from a mental and emotional standpoint, I didn't know if I had the strength to go through with it especially faced with opposition from my family. Hopelessly, I let lawyer papers fall through my hands and let time carry away any tiny shred of justice.

64

Something in me broke. I grappled unsuccessfully with severe negativism and lack of confidence and trust in myself.

I had mistakenly believed that dating Yi was a good idea because I was focused on improving my Chinese language mastery and emotional maturity. I had believed that college would improve my life through freedom and independence from Mom and Dad. I thought the MBA would get me a better job and better life. I had worked on my relationship intelligence and made small or big steps in improving my quality of relationship each time, but my relationships had fallen apart. I had taken a stand and followed the company outlined steps to report something wrong that had been done to me.

On the one hand, I felt I was trying my hardest and I should be proud of that. On the other hand, all I could see was that I had possibly just made the worst financial decision of my life. I had quit as opposed to being fired so I was told I couldn't even collect unemployment benefits.

To make matters worse, I had a mortgage that bled away at my financial savings. My rainy day funds had been funneled into Joe already and I didn't have high hopes of seeing that money again at this point. Mom and Dad were absolutely positive that I was the stupidest human being on the planet for quitting from Chevron. The nickname I had earned as a child, "piece of shit", seemed more apt than ever.

At first, that made me sad and more depressed, but then when I accepted that I was truly a "piece of shit", it was freeing in a way. Being a "piece of shit" meant that I didn't have to meet their standards anymore; after all, what was the point? If I didn't want to be a "piece of shit", I had to conform to their norms and standards, but if I was just a "piece of shit", then I wasn't part of their system anymore. After all a "piece of shit" couldn't be expected to do anything with their life.

It was a massive, almost hysterical relief. After taking inventory on how long my existing funds would last me, I fully relaxed and spent long days just playing video games in my pajamas. Although I knew my financial obligations would eventually become an issue, I felt it was important to take some time to truly recover. In my planning and scheduling I gave myself space to unwind as well as time to make sure I met my responsibilities. I let real life fall away from me.

For the first time in my life, I felt free. I had no boss. I was on the other side of the world from Mom and Dad. I was not in a relationship; it was just me, my pets, and I. I ate when I wanted, dressed how I wanted, did what I wanted. I channeled all my energy into creating a healthy and happy me. I cut out the outside world, decorating my home on a budget. I returned to my habit of reading. I focused on learning how to cook better and challenged myself with new recipes. This was enjoyable, both as a mental pursuit as well as very tasty. I exercised regularly and went on adventures with my dogs.

I was happy, but as time went by, I felt more and more that life was too good to be true—and it was. My savings could only last for so long.

65

Dad, always more gracious with money than with affection, offered to pay the mortgage for one year. The funds necessary to pay for my small starter home for one year was not a huge cost to him.

More importantly, we both knew it would give him power over me again. I would feel beholden to him because of the money, and he would feel that I owed him at least some level of obedience. I did not want to return to being his person, his thing to command to do this or that, and I knew the money would make him feel he had the right to do that. But I didn't want to lose the house, so he wired me the funds.

A couple months later, Mom and Dad let me know they were coming over for Christmas and New Year's. I tried my best to keep things civil. I hoped that if I could make them happy, perhaps they would be less abusive.

I cleared out of the master bedroom and arranged to sleep on an air mattress during their stay. I let them use my car when they pleased. I carefully dressed the way they liked me to be dressed, avoiding any pants and opting for long skirts so that Mom would not have to see my body. She still felt that at one hundred and twenty-seven pounds, I was disgusting. I listened quietly as they lectured me on my sleep schedule and other lifestyle habits. I let them criticize anything and everything about me. I let them re-organize most of my house.

Through all this, I asked only one thing, that they not reorganize the kitchen.

They demanded that I cook my best dishes for the family for New Year's Eve. Cooking was something I did out of love, and I felt no love right now; only a black, dark hatred that I could not fully suppress. I had a thin skin of control wrapped around it all and I crossed my fingers that nothing would threaten it further.

I took a deep breath and went to the kitchen to begin cooking for the family. It was while I was in the kitchen that I realized Mom and Dad had done the one small thing I had asked them not to do. Dishes, pots, and pans had been moved. Utensils were no longer in the same drawer.

I stared in shock. I had hoped that—just this one time, with this one request—they would listen to me. I was thunderstruck. I cooked the meal in a fog.

As I was serving out the fruits of my labor, a casual comment that Dad made about his perceptions and opinions of my laziness sliced dangerously into my sanity. Inside, I felt a strange pain, and the shock of it led me to do something I had not been able to bring myself to do before.

[No more.]

I set the soup down very gently and heard myself calmly explain that Mom and Dad were going to move out to a hotel. Tonight. Then I braced for the explosion this statement would surely cause.

There was a moment of silence. I had never talked like this before. When they recovered from their surprise, Dad hurled every verbal assault he could muster at me, bellowing that I was the worst daughter in all of history. I was the worst nightmare, a monster, spawn of Satan, and other things. Mom screamed her own insults and dragged out any ugliness of the past she felt could illustrate her words. I was the most undesirable, unforgivable, most worthless human being in the world. I should go to hell.

I nodded and felt a distant pity as I watched them. Mom even brought up my suicide attempt from when I was eighteen as evidence explaining why I was a bad daughter because of all those hospital bills. She also ranted about other times I had let her down. She wailed that she should have known then that I was a traitorous monster.

They demanded that I not only owed them the money they had lent me for the mortgage payments, but for my whole life as well. They stated that I owed them from the moment I was mistakenly conceived. That I owed them for every penny they spent on me since birth, but as one last favor to me, they would settle for $600,000. They announced that they did not want me anymore and that I'd better pay them back.

I stared blankly ahead and didn't refute anything they were saying. Mom and Dad ranted and screamed, but could not break my outward calm.

Angrily, they flung clothes into suitcases while they cursed my existence. I let all their words clatter to the floor around me like the rapidly unburdened clothes hangers. They could snarl whatever they wanted, but I was kicking them out of my house now—out of my life.

They slammed the door shut, and it was several long minutes before I went over to lock it.

And so ended December 31st, 2016. We didn't make it to New Year's.

I have not contacted or seen them since.

Epilogue

I was raised in an environment that didn't educate me about what abuse was. This kept me trapped as a victim of abuse wherever I went because I didn't know better and because I was told that if it felt bad it was my fault. I was raised to doubt my own emotions, perceptions, and decisions and to trust instead in my abusers.

For years, my greatest desire was to hurt my abusers back as deeply as they had hurt me (especially my parents). I found what liberated me was digging myself out of hatred and anger and focusing on what matters most.

Since kicking them out, I have dedicated my energy to building a fulfilling life for myself. On my own, I've proved to myself that I do have value and worth in this world. I've finally learned to stand on my own and stand up for myself. I have finally broken free from toxic relationships, a toxic work environment, and a toxic family.

I've learned the definition of the word "rape" and other abuse-related terminology as well as coping mechanisms and mental health measures that I have taken to claw my way into living a normal, healthy life.

I don't expect life to be rainbows and butterflies, and it definitely hasn't been, but I know with certainty that I will find my way.

For my thirtieth birthday, I decided to publish this book.

Thank you for reading my story.

www.ingramcontent.com/pod-product-compliance
Lightning Source LLC
Chambersburg PA
CBHW020403080526
44584CB00014B/1156